DARKNESS INTO LIGHT

Ascendancy

DARKNESS INTO LIGHT

Rescuing Souls on the Other Side

JOHN L. BROOKER

BLUE DOLPHIN

Published by Blue Dolphin Publishing, Inc.
P.O. Box 8, Nevada City, CA 95959
Orders: 1-800-643-0765
Web: www.bluedolphinpublishing.com

ISBN: 1-57733-094-3

Library of Congress Cataloging-in-Publication Data

Brooker, John L., 1923–
     Darkness into light : rescuing souls on the other side /
John L. Brooker.
        p. cm.
      ISBN 1-57733-094-3
      1. Spiritualism. 2. Death—Miscellanea. I. Title

   BF1275.D2 B75 2001
   133.9—dc21

                                                      2001035185

Cover illustration by John Linn, "Ascendancy"
Cover design by Verena Shayani
Cover typography design by Jeff Case

Printed in the United States of America

10   9   8   7   6   5   4   3   2

TABLE OF CONTENTS

ACKNOWLEDGMENTS

MOST OF THE PEOPLE I wish to thank are in the world of Spirit. They are the guides and teachers who have inspired this work and have always helped with their information and encouragement. I also thank them for the opportunity to be of service to those souls who were lost in the astral planes.

There have been many mediums who have given their time and devotion to rescue work without reward except for the thanks of those they have helped to find their way home to the spirit world. These include Cheryl, Elizabeth, Florence, Joye, Juliana, Lorraine, Marsha, Phyllis, Sharon, Verena, Viola, and Viretta. I would like to thank Joan Hatley, and Jim and Marti Reynolds for helping with the development of the manuscript.

My apologies to anyone I have omitted.

I also thank and respect all those mediums who I have had guidance from. The many sittings I had over the years gave me the evidence I needed to give me the assurance of survival of the human spirit beyond the grave.

Mostly, I wish to thank my wife Naomi for proofreading and correcting the manuscript as it developed. Also, I thank her for her patience over the many years I have been involved in my pursuit of the truth. Without her love and encouragement this book would not have been written.

INTRODUCTION

ONE DAY, IN 1949, I stopped for a late lunch at an unfamiliar restaurant in London, and that lunch changed my life. A surprising series of coincidences began, and I often look back and marvel at the sequence of events that occurred.

The proprietor of the restaurant was being teased in a friendly way about ghosts and spirits by some of the customers. When they left, I asked him what that was all about, and he told me he was a Spiritualist. I asked him what that was, and he told me he believed in life after death and communication with spirit people. He told me there was an extensive religion on the subject and there were churches throughout England. He was so enthusiastic about it that I thought I would look into it.

He gave me a schedule of activities at the Spiritualist Association of Great Britain (SAGB) in Belgrave Square and suggested I visit there if I was interested. I left the restaurant and later found myself in Belgrave Square. I was told of a public meeting on the following Sunday, and if I attended I would learn more about Spiritualism.

I attended the meeting and there were about 300 people in this big hall. A man gave a talk about parapsychology and metaphysics using words I had never heard before. His main theme was that the occult was the only way to discover truth. As I had no idea what he was talking about, I was rather bored with his speech.

Then came a medium named Ena Twigg on to the platform. She said, "I don't usually do this, but there is an Arab guide marching up and down the center aisle, insisting I speak to a man named Brooks."

Two other people in the hall knew someone of that name, but she said it was not for them. She said the person she wanted had recently returned from Australia, and, as I had just been there, I raised my hand. She was quite annoyed that I had taken so long to respond. She could not know this was my first experience of this subject and I did not know about mediums and Arab guides.

She proceeded to tell me about some family members in spirit as well as some personal information she could not possibly have known about. Most of the information about the relatives in spirit I had to confirm with my mother as I had no knowledge of them. All of the names checked out and the personal information, including a prediction, was amazingly accurate.

This whole experience intrigued me; so, I attended the meeting the following week. This time there was a man named Harold Sharp giving a very impassioned talk about the atom bombing of Nagasaki and Hiroshima and the hundreds of thousands of people suddenly being sent to spirit.

As I watched him, there appeared a beautiful white light which completely enshrouded him. Around the light there were circles of brilliant color. In the middle of this light there was a beautiful face and it was impossible to tell whether it was a male or female. I thought everyone could see what I was seeing but apparently this was not so. I left there wondering what Spiritualism was all about, and why was I able to see the vision.

During the following week I joined the SAGB and saw Harold Sharp in the tea room. I approached him and told him what I had seen and he was surprised. He had received a letter that day from a man who had also attended the meeting. This man was an insurance salesman who was inspired to buy an easel and some paints. He would set up the easel and canvas and meditate. When he came out of his meditation he would find a completed painting on the canvas.

When the man went home after the meeting he had been entranced by a spirit who had been an artist on earth and he had painted a portrait. Harold Sharp said that from my description it may be the same person that I had seen at the meeting. He gave me the letter, I contacted the artist and the portrait was identical to what I had seen. The artist's name was John Linn and he called the portrait "Ascendancy" (see front cover).

John and I met a few times and his artist guide painted a portrait of my mother whom John had never met. Again the likeness was uncanny. More coincidences.

A few months later I attended a materialization seance where people from spirit could manifest in full form. The first person to materialize was John Linn and he told me he had a heart attack and had died suddenly. I was deeply shocked as I had no idea he was sick. I confirmed his passing but could not trace the disposition of his paintings.

I began to read as much as I could on the subject. I had a number of sittings with a variety of mediums and was repeatedly told I would be involved deeply in Spiritualism. This was surprising as I was never interested in religion of any kind. However, I found that Spiritualism appealed to me because I felt comfortable with their teachings. It includes people of all faiths and has a very broad philosophy. The principles are based on the simple truth of survival of the human spirit, as well as the Golden Rule for human behavior. I think the greatest appeal for me is the fact that they teach that God is a force of creative energy and love and not some superhuman being.

I began to study the New Testament again and realized I was seeing it from a new perspective. The Sermon on the Mount has taken on a new significance and has mystical qualities I had not seen before. Now, each time I read it I see more truth emerging.

I joined Harold Sharp's development circle and met his wonderful guide, Brother Peter. Harold was a trance medium, which means he was able to go into trance and Brother Peter could impress Harold with what to say. Brother Peter gave lectures through Harold on the healing qualities of herbs and also some enlightening philosophical talks on life after death.

This was all strange to me but I soon learned of the many ways that spirit can communicate with us on earth. Harold had been a Monk at one time, but left the monastery after seeing some wonderful visions, which led him to a more direct service to mankind offered by Spiritualism.

This association with Harold Sharp and Brother Peter led me into a series of amazing experiences. Under Harold's guidance, I became a healer and was able to experience the flow of healing energy that came from spirit to help people in need. I was privileged to become a healer at the SAGB for about five years.

There have been many famous people who were members of the SAGB. One prominent member was Arthur Conan Doyle, the author of the Sherlock Holmes mysteries. He had lost his son, Raymond, during the war, and Raymond had materialized to his parents at a seance in

Wales. After the meeting Doyle said he would not write any more fiction when the book he was writing was finished, and would devote his time to Spiritualism. In the book he was writing he killed off Holmes and his arch enemy Moriarty. There was such an outcry from his readers that he had to resurrect them two years later. He was so deeply impressed with the evidence he had received that his life was changed. He became a strong supporter of Spiritualism for the remainder of his life and wrote some books on the subject.

From the wide variety of mediums I have sat with I was able to witness many different kinds of phenomena. The one medium who impressed me the most was Leslie Flint. He would sit with me singly, or with a small group, and voices from spirit would come out of the air. He would be fully conscious and would take part in the sitting. He was what is called a direct voice medium and he used no paraphernalia in his work. If at any time Spirit could not communicate because of adverse conditions, there was never a fee.

Many guides and relatives would come to speak to me and I received some amazing evidence through Leslie Flint's mediumship. Many famous people had sittings with him. He was tested by many different scientific groups and he was always cleared of any wrongdoing. He only charged a minimal fee for his work and he had great faith in his guides.

Brother Peter told me there is guide who is always with me from the world of spirit. His name is Bishop Abbot Jocelin of Bath and Wells. He lived in the eleventh century and was responsible for the building of Wells Cathedral in Somerset.

I went to Wells in Somerset and was able to find much evidence of Jocelin and his life. He was signatory of the

Magna Carta and he crowned Henry III the boy king. I never felt any psychic impressions from Jocelin at Wells and realized later that he had probably lost interest in his past life after 800 years in the spirit world. I believe he did not want me to think of his past life, rather that I should concentrate more on the present

I have learned much from my studies of this subject, and I have had irrefutable evidence of the survival of the human soul after the change called death. I know the next life is merely another state of awareness which we can communicate with. I know there are specially gifted people who can tune into this other world and bring evidence of survival to us.

I know that consciousness is the primary creative force in life and it manifests to us as love. There is a love within us that can be developed and can link us with the great creative force we call God. I know that no one is ever completely lost and there are many wonderful souls waiting to help us if we need it. I soon found that many souls do need help when they leave this earth because they are not aware they have died or are hiding for some reason.

During all this research, I met my wife Naomi, an American visiting England. On one of our first dates I took her to a seance. This was a trumpet seance where megaphones floated around the room and were used to magnify the voices from spirit. Next to us, two of the trumpets were used for a three-way discussion with a lady. The two people in spirit began an argument over some date in the past. This fascinated me, and I suddenly realized there was a pain in my hand and Naomi's nails were digging into my palm. I had forgotten to warn her of what would happen and I think she was more than a little nervous! Not any more, she has been a great support to me in this work.

It was at this meeting I was told that I would be going to another country. When I asked which country the guide just said, "It is across the water." I had just returned from a trip to Australia so I assumed that was where I was going. As things transpired I married Naomi two years later and we came to America in 1961.

I have been conducting groups for spiritual and psychic development and lecturing on this subject for many years, and I became a Spiritualist Minister in 1977. Many people have developed their psychic abilities in the groups I have conducted, and out of the groups I have been guided into doing what is called Rescue Work.

With the help of many trance mediums I have been able to help a lot of people who have died but did not know it. There are several reasons for a person not to know they have died, and they need help to be made aware of their situation. They need help to find their relatives and friends who have preceded them.

This book was suggested by guides from the spirit world, and I have felt some strong spiritual influences during the writing of it. Each chapter is to stand alone, and only my personal experiences are to be discussed.

The purpose of the book is to help people understand what happens when we die. There is plenty of evidence in the examples of rescue work, of survival beyond this life, and there are some comments from teachers and guides in spirit.

The knowledge that we survive this life should not be a fearful thing but a relief that there is some reason and purpose for this worldly experience. Similarly, the thought that there is something wonderful to follow this life and that death is not the end, should be comforting.

CHAPTER ONE

COMMUNICATION WITH SPIRIT

M OST RELIGIONS TEACH that there is some form of life
after death; however, in Spiritualism they go a step
further and explore this truth by trying to pierce the
apparent veil between the two worlds. Spiritualists take
survival beyond the grave as a fact and try to confirm this
truth by communication with the so-called dead. This is
achieved by specially gifted people called mediums who
have the ability to get information from those who have
made the transition before us.

Throughout the years, there have always been people
who have the ability to communicate with the spirit world,
and the Bible has many examples of such people. The God
force speaks to man through the Saints, spirit guides and
other intermediaries to bring the message of our divine
heritage to us.

This link with the next world can occur to anyone who
is open to such influences, and most people have had some
kind of inexplicable spiritual or psychic incident in their
lives, especially when they are praying. Most people do not
usually talk about this for fear of being ridiculed. Although,
most people will have something to contribute if the subject of other world contacts is raised. Persons in the spirit

world can be closely attuned to us on the earth when they wish and our loved ones often do so. Love appears to be the one emotion that can cross the barriers.

Many people have been and are very conscious of a departed loved one's presence. This presence is often very comforting for a grieving person. The soul in spirit is aware of the grief of the one left behind and will draw close to try to bring comfort. Unfortunately the presence of the one in spirit is a reminder of their past life together, and that brings sadness.

It is a basic teaching of Spiritualism that we are a spiritual being temporarily expressing ourselves through a physical body, and when we die we continue life in another world. This spirit world appears to be a duplicate of the earth plane and we recreate our surroundings based on our memories of the earth plane existence.

Once we have adjusted to the new vibration we continue learning, changing and growing as we do here. We do not suddenly become angels sitting on a cloud playing a harp, nor is there a judgment day. We create our own reality wherever we direct our attention, whether in this dimension or out-of-body. There is no angry God waiting to punish us for being human; we have to live with who we think we are and deal with our own guilt.

I understand from the teachings I have received, that before we are born into this world we are appointed a guide who will be with us throughout this life. They are mostly unseen, but many people have recorded how they have felt some guidance and protection in moments of crisis. Many people have had a moment of spontaneous clairvoyance and have seen into the next world. I have had some experience of such visions.

We each have a guide who will stay with us through the intervening planes between the earth and the spirit world. A person may have more than one guide, depending on the tasks he may have set for himself before he is born. We have usually known these guides for long periods of time before we are born, and they have agreed to help us in our quest for experience in this world. They will help us reach self-fulfillment, which is to outgrow our wish to be in this dimension.

People in spirit who wish to communicate with this world have to adapt to the conditions here. Similarly, mediums have to raise their sensitivity to the level of the next plane which they are trying to contact. Anyone from spirit is limited in this world and must use the services of a medium's energy field to communicate. Spirit people do not have physical eyes to see into this world. They are able to know what we are thinking and can sense what we are experiencing, by our emotional reaction to what is happening around us.

Apparently, all communication is by mental telepathy and is done by concepts, not in words. The mind of the medium will translate the concept into the language we know, regardless of the basic language of both the person on earth and the person in spirit. This must be how one of the great beings in spirit can send a universal message which we can all enjoy. I have heard languages spoken by mediums in trance which I know the medium does not understand, but usually one of the listeners will know the language.

I once was spoken to by an American Indian in a language I had never heard. I tried to get the tape translated but was told it was probably a dead language (excuse the pun).

When coming to us from another level, a spirit person must first adjust his vibration to that of the energy level of this plane. Once the vibration levels are compatible the guide can speak through a medium. A guide is not always limited by the vocabulary and intellect of the medium. He can find things in the mind of the medium that will allow him to convey anything he wishes to say. It is not the words he is searching for; rather, it is the ideas or concepts that he wishes to get across to the listeners.

As all communication from the spirit world is by thought transference, and thought is like a radio wave, we have only to tune into the higher frequency to get the message. Prayer or meditation can raise our awareness to that higher frequency and two-way communication can be established.

The purpose of the guides coming here is to bring us their wisdom and enlightenment. Sometimes a person can be conscious of the presence of spirit beings because they have an atmosphere which is different from ours. They have a very bright light and a strong energy field vibration surrounding them. The atmosphere created by their presence will be beneficial to us even if their words are not heard or understood. The power they have and bring with them knows nothing but purity, nothing but love, and we cannot help but benefit from the atmosphere they create. We all project a light from within us and the more spiritual person will have a much brighter light.

Some of the guides who come to us have lived on the earth before, some have not. So it is easier for some of them to draw closer to the earth atmosphere. If the spirit has lived on the earth before, they can identify with the vibration of the life they knew at that time. Of course, having been gone for such a long time, the more advanced souls cannot recall anything but good, anything but beauty. It seems that as we withdraw from this life, we begin to outgrow many of the attachments we think are so important here, and eventually we become more pure as a total being.

It is only on the earth plane that we distinguish between good and evil. Good is what we approve of, and evil is what we disapprove of. It is only our judgment or opinion of a situation that determines our feelings, and in the final analysis we decide our priorities. We may break a speed limit when we think our priorities require it and feel justified in doing so.

One teacher once said to me, "I am here to make you realize your capabilities. You are not different from me if you take away the physical body. Your knowledge is not less than mine, it is only that you live in a restrictive world. You live in a world where everything appears difficult, and you have to work harder to obtain the knowledge than you are not less than I am. You have all come through many experiences and you have more knowledge than you give yourselves credit.

"You all have the knowledge and the opportunity to serve mankind in many ways. Remember we are with you and will send you the thoughts that will help, and more importantly, we send you the great power of love. So go out into the earth plane and let your love and light blossom. Have no fear that your knowledge will not be received. People may not be ready to receive it at this time, but they will eventually understand what you have implanted in their subconscious."

He told me that guides do not have absolute power as they cannot penetrate into our personal atmosphere without our permission. We all have a boundary around us which is our protection, and no one enters into this area except our guides who were appointed and have been given that permission.

Prior to coming to this world we have agreed to do some things for mankind in the name of spirit. The appropriate guides were chosen, and they are the ones who have priority as regards communication and control over who is eligible to come close to us from the spirit world. The purpose of the guide is not to change the atmosphere of the medium, but only to pass on some knowledge of the life to come and the reassurance that we will all survive this life.

A guide will try to respond to any request of the individual that is to the ultimate good of the person. However, they cannot, and will not, interfere with a person's free will. They have no wish to try to live vicariously through anyone on the earth plane. There was once a theory around that people from spirit could take over the body of a dying person and continue to live on earth. They were called "Walk ins".

I once asked a guide about this possibility, and if there was such a thing as spirit possession - where a person from spirit took over the body of someone on earth. He said, "Do you honestly think anyone from spirit would want to leave the beauty here, and enter the body of a sick or dying person on the earth plane? You are totally inviolate, a unique individual."

He went on to explain that we confuse obsession with possession. A person who cannot face a life situation on earth may assume a totally different identity and become obsessed with the new personality. This is a mental health situation and has nothing to do with Spiritualism.

There have been many cases of multiple personalities, and in my professional capacity as a Social Worker and as a rescue worker, I have never seen a case of spirit possession. Some people blame spirit for their misbehavior and claim the "Devil made me do it." There is no Devil or hell.

Spontaneous communication does take place. When two people have been very close for a number of years, and one of them goes to spirit, the remaining person will often be aware of the presence of their loved one. Sometimes the one in spirit is drawn close by the distress of the one on earth. They would like to reassure the person that they are all right and have found a wonderful sense of peace, free of any sickness or pain.

Love will always penetrate the barrier between the worlds in both directions. How nice it would be if survival was common knowledge, and we could all enjoy direct communication with our loved ones in spirit. There is so much to be learned by us here on the earth plane. It is wonderful to know that communication does take place, and our messages to our loved ones are received, as are our prayers to a higher level of consciousness.

One guide told me that guides are persons who have been in spirit for a long time. He said, "Do not think your guide may not be able to understand your needs. They have access to the most advanced souls in the spirit world, and your guide can act as a channel for information from the highest sources if they need to."

Usually our loved ones are not capable of being guides to the ones they have left behind. They are obviously emotionally involved and would try to influence us and not allow free will and the natural growth process to proceed. I think we need our challenges to teach us our strengths and weaknesses,.

I have spoken to many guides and helpers throughout the years and have received much help and advice from them. They have given many talks about life in spirit and have removed any fears of the necessary transition we all must make. I know I have many helpers in the spirit world because of the rescue work I am involved in. I am often aware of the presence of my guides when I am discussing spiritual matters and especially when I am working with terminally ill patients.

I volunteer as a Hospice worker and have the opportunity to discuss the transition process with some patients who have a fear of dying. Many patients who are near death will begin to see loved ones from spirit who have come to meet them. It is as if there is a withdrawal process taking place, and I try to reassure them that they are not crazy or hallucinating.

These situations provide me with an opportunity to let them know there is nothing to fear and that death is like going to sleep and waking up in another world where there is nothing but love and freedom from pain and suffering.

I try to get them to understand that sickness dies with the physical body and they will have a completely new life experience in a duplicate spirit body as they outgrow any attachments to this world. The truth of survival of the human spirit is really all a person needs to know. The loved ones or the workers in spirit will do all that is necessary to help anyone coming over.

For those who have lost a loved one previously, the idea of a reunion in spirit is very appealing. I try to explain the process they will go through when they go to join their loved ones and let them know there is nothing to fear.

I tell them to send out a thought to their loved ones when they leave this earth and they will appear and help them to adjust to the new conditions.

As all communication from spirit to the earth plane has to pass through the mind-brain system of a medium there is usually some influence of the medium's personality and vocabulary in the message coming through. Most mediums are able to sublimate most of their influence and they try not to interfere with the message.

In rescue work the mediums are usually very deeply entranced and are not aware of most of the proceedings. In fact most of them would rather not know some of the gory details of the respondent's problems. Of course, not all souls coming through have serious problems. Many souls just want permission to go on but are not aware of what to do.

During the past two years there has come a new type of rescue work mediumship. Two mediums are now partially conscious during the session and can participate to some degree in the process. They cannot work directly with the person coming through, but they are aware of their presence. Unfortunately I cannot be sure how much input is coming from the medium in this case.

CHAPTER TWO

THE POWER OF PRAYER

W HEN OUR THOUGHTS TAKE WING and we reach for a higher power, we are asking to have a conversation with our own higher self. Regardless of the way humanity sees this higher force, or by whatever name it is given at this time, most people have a belief in a higher power. It is remarkable in this materialistic Western world, where we are inundated with a diet of sex and violence from the media, that trust in such a force persists. Perhaps we need an outlet through prayer to offset this barrage of negative suggestions.

Many people in our culture have a cynicism where a higher power is concerned, that is, until they feel the need of some reassurance. When in a life-threatening situation, they often renew a faith in a supreme being and pray for help. I believe there are few atheists in the cancer or AIDS wards, as well as on the battlefields.

True prayer does not have to be a well-rehearsed ritualistic recitation to be mumbled like a shopping list. It should be a very private declaration from the heart. It need not contain any words at all, it could be an attitude shift toward a more spiritual life. The realization of the divine presence in our life creates a loving, spiritual, frame of reference, from which we can live in accord with higher principles.

Anytime we raise our thoughts in appreciation of a beautiful scene, or hear a song of praise to God, it can be like a prayer of thanks for being alive. Sitting quietly and letting the mind wander in a spiritual reverie can bring a peaceful feeling of being in touch with a higher force. Many people have felt a sense of unity with nature, or, of being in touch with another reality when alone and free of stress.

For some people religion and prayer are matters of expediency, only to be used in an emergency. However, life has a habit of providing those situations that appear to require some acceptance of, or intervention from, a higher power. These incidents make us aspire to higher powers and such surrender of the intellect is good for our growth.

The use of prayer as a link between the self and a supreme being brings a warm, compassionate, loving presence into our lives. It brings the reassurance of the closeness of a divine influence in the scheme of things. We can draw on that presence for healing for ourselves and others, and we can secretly ask for divine intervention in our life. We can learn the true nature of unconditional love by simply raising our consciousness in prayer. Prayer is a matter of the heart, which is the source of love, both physical and spiritual.

For me, prayer is an attitude of hopefulness, a natural human response acknowledging the life force flowing through my veins. I feel prayer brings access to the answers to all those basic questions and mysteries of life.

It is natural to ask for help from this source of love for we can become aware of its presence when in a meditative state or a state of complete surrender of the self to a divine presence. When we become closer to the source of this power in prayer or meditation, we can know that there is a basic energy, or force of love, that is the source of all things created. It is in these inner planes of awareness that we recognize that love is the primary characteristic of this creative essence that we lovingly call the God force.

Hundreds of religious groups have been formed; so there is a wide variety of interpretations of this supreme force. From the "Hell fire and damnation" churches, through the ritualistic religions, through such philosophies as Yoga and Parapsychology, it seems impossible to find a common thread. Perhaps the use of prayer and the recognition that there is a supreme force is the thread that ties the various facets of religion together.

To me, Spiritualism seems to be the most practical of the religions I have studied. All religions teach some form of belief in an afterlife, and the presence of a superior creative force in life. It seems they are all asking the same questions in different ways. Spiritualism goes one step further. It teaches that not only is there an afterlife, but also it is possible and desirable, to communicate with those planes of consciousness.

Spiritualists ask souls in spirit for help in understanding the nature of life after death, and they call on those advanced souls for answers to those intriguing questions about who and what we are, and what life will be like when we make our own transition. There is a feeling of peace that comes with such knowledge. The assurance that there is an extension of life into another dimension removes the greatest fear from our lives. The fear of death no longer has any meaning for there is no death.

One of the most popular uses of prayer is to ask for help in the healing of other people. It is one of the aspects of spiritual healing and is called absent healing. It consists of linking in with a person who is sick and asking for some divine influence to heal them. Some churches have groups of people who will gather together to send healing to people who have requested help. The groups will have healing lists which are usually open for anyone to add their name.

This practice of absent healing makes people aware of the power of prayer and helps them to raise their thoughts to a higher source for help. If the person receiving the healing prayer is aware of what is happening, then the psychological benefit helps both patient and healer.

In England, after World War II, a spiritual healer named Harry Edwards discovered it took exactly one minute for Big Ben, the clock on the Houses of Parliament in London, to play the Westminster Chimes, and strike the hour of nine o'clock.

For many years the BBC used these chimes as an introduction to the nine o'clock news. Harry Edwards called on all healers to send out healing for anyone who was sick, and the sick were to tune in to receive healing at that time. This became popular as the healing minute. Then, when the BBC introduced an electronic beep to introduce the news, there was such an outcry that they reinstated the chimes.

An atheist or cynic might say that if it is true that there is a supreme, all-knowing, all-powerful force directing things on this planet, then prayer is not necessary - especially when it is used to intercede in someone else's life. It is, after all, reminding God that he has forgotten someone. Such cynicism sees God as a person and ignores the value of faith in a supreme force. The many spontaneous healings that have taken place as a result of the psychological power of prayer justify its use.

Prayer is a declaration of hope for better things in the future and proclaims an intent to interact with a supreme deity. It helps a person escape from the mundane of everyday life and feel in touch with a comforting force.

There can be great emotional support for the lonely and despairing in this life, and there is a need for comfort for those in need.

Meditation is a form of prayer and, like prayer, meditation can be practiced in private. I like to encourage people to meditate and link in to a higher part of their being and find that peace of mind that comes from the practice of meditation.

In some meditation practice, there is a form of prayer in the use of a repeated word or phrase which is called a mantra. This will bring a hypnotic state of mind and permit the user to focus his attention inwardly to discover his inner self.

The use of a mantra is a common practice in the religions of the Eastern nations, and many people use the term, "OM." This term is the name of the creative, divine force and brings the meditator in touch with the infinite.

One mantra that I have found works well for people in the Western world is "I AM." This will lead to an internal review of ones self-identity and will lead to access to an inner level of awareness. All one has to do is to prepare for meditation in the usual way then mentally repeat the term "I AM." It will soon become a blur which will closely resemble the term, "OM."

It helps if you visualize you are in the center of a beacon that projects light in every direction; however, you are the center of this force of creation. Try to hold the image of yourself as the source of light. Let yourself relax and surrender to the light and let it take you into other levels of experience.

Linking in to the creative force through prayer will bring the experience known as "The descent of grace." It is a blessing which will bring the realization of the oneness of all things.

The state of Grace is a total experience of a divine force that seems to descend from the top of the head. It sweeps down through the body permeating every cell. A person is left with a feeling of bliss and contentment. The meditator takes on a feeling of being one with the whole creation. All mankind is seen as one, and we are all part of the creative essence. Light seems to emanate from the heart and surround the body.

The feeling of ecstacy that accompanies this experience can last for hours. Unfortunately, we cannot live at such an exalted state of being, but the trip is well worth the endeavor. Once this state of grace is experienced there are no more questions, but a knowing and acceptance of the divine power that flows through us and creates us and all that is.

If a person realizes that he has the ability and power to use prayer as a blessing, he can surround himself with a radiance and energy of spiritual power. He can create an aura of peace and tranquility that others will notice from his presence. This presence will attract those in need, to seek him out for counsel and advice and he will have the pleasure of doing a service to mankind.

Having a spiritual presence does not mean wearing a long face and carrying a Bible under the arm. It means we radiate the vitality of the universe which is creativity and love and joy. We are here to bring on earth the love of God, and prayer is the channel to bring it to us.

CHAPTER THREE

TRANSITION TO SPIRIT:
Darkness into Light

THROUGHOUT THIS LIFE we are often reminded of the inevitable transition we must make to the next world. To many people, what happens when we make this change is one of the big mysteries for which there are many conflicting theories. Many people believe that death is the end and feel there is no point in believing otherwise. Evidence to the contrary will not deter them from this belief and they will have to wait until they leave this earth to learn the truth. In rescue work I meet many who do not want to accept the truth of survival even though they are dead in the eyes of this world and they are alive and speaking to me.

There have been several recent studies of people who have had near death experiences where they were declared clinically dead; then, they have recovered to live many more productive years. When the transition took place, they nearly all had a similar experience. They had the sensation of rising up out of the body and being aware of the room where they were. They then found they were moving up toward a very bright light, and they nearly all had a very clear picture of someone coming to meet them out of the light.

During the out-of-body period there was a total absence of fear, and the person coming to meet them, sometimes a relative, seemed to project a wonderful feeling of love to them. There was some telepathic communication between them, and some were told they had to return to earth to fulfill some purpose. Some were aware of the choice of returning to earth or staying in spirit. Those that survived obviously made the decision to return to this life to report this phenomenon.

Each person having this experience had a change in his beliefs about life, and each reported that they now had no fear of death. They all knew they had lived on in another dimension and had the same feelings of self-awareness as they did on earth. The one feeling they all shared was the tremendous power of love and total acceptance that came from the beings they met.

Most religions profess to know the secrets of what happens to us when we die. However, to me Spiritualism seems to have the most sensible interpretation of the transition. Some religions teach that the afterlife is one where we are judged and punished for any wrongdoing during our lives on earth. Spiritualism teaches there is a continuation of life on the other side of the veil and the only punishment is that which is self-created.

What may be called punishment is usually guilt caused by the realization that apparent past misdeeds have caused problems back on earth that resulted from such behavior. These people are helped by rescue workers to free themselves from this guilt. The guilt carried by a mass murderer is inconceivable to us and the fact that there is no escape from the memory of his behavior means he will probably create a hell for himself. One of the worst punishments is the fact that he cannot die and end the memory of his behavior.

A rescue worker is someone on the earth plane who uses the services of a trance medium. These mediums allow persons who have died, to receive help in order to progress from what is called the astral plane to the spirit world. The astral plane is called the emotion and desire plane for here people are able to outgrow many of their earth related attachments.

Each person who dies has to come to the realization that life continues and that his ideas about reality will have to adjust to the new dimension in which he finds himself. His perceptions about who and what he is have to change, and this change must come from within. Consequently, there is much soul searching and self-recrimination as these changes take place. This sense of guilt causes the most hardened criminal to hide in darkness and suffer self-inflicted punishment. Many of them would like to return to earth to correct some of the damage they have done. I generally tell them that the past is dead and there is nothing they can do about it.

It is difficult for people on the earth plane to accept the truth that there is no judgment or punishment as we are always measuring ourselves up against other people. This is a form of judgment of other people. We believe some criteria of what is right and we set up impossible expectations for ourselves and others around us. We have to learn that sin is only someone else's opinion of our behavior.

No one, regardless of their supposed transgressions, is ever completely lost and no one is cast into some hell. There is no such place, nor is there purgatory. Many Catholics firmly believe there is such a place, but it is easy for a rescue worker to help them see the truth that this is church doctrine and not necessarily true. There is always help for anyone who is ready to accept it.

When some people die and think they have committed wrongs on earth and then realize there is no death, they will try to hide. They will devise some elaborate protective screens to avoid detection, not realizing there are no secrets in the spirit world and there is no place to hide. They will mentally try to maintain their identity on earth and refuse to accept guidance from anyone in spirit trying to help them. Unless a person can raise his consciousness away from his problem and the earth plane, he will still be attached to his beliefs about the reality of the earth plane life.

People who have no concept of an afterlife will recreate a situation they can recall from their last memory on earth. This will usually limit their ability to progress to a higher plane for a while, where their loved ones are waiting for them. For example, a person who is trapped in a car, a burning building, or has drowned, may continue to think of his situation as real and will need to be rescued. His belief in his condition and the exercise of his free will, precludes any help from the guides in spirit getting through to him. However, the guides can always influence him to link up with a rescue worker on the earth plane.

As I am still on earth, people who are trapped will open up and relate to me. For example, a man came through who had been trapped in a mine cave-in. No one knew he was there and he believed he was doomed to die there, which he did. I told him I could pull him out and created an illusion of an escape route. He had been in there for some months but he thought it was just a couple of days.

Many souls are concerned that their passing would not be known to significant people on earth. A homosexual prostitute in San Francisco told me he had been picked up and taken by a client to Oakland, California where he died in a fire. He was worried that no one knew he had gone to Oakland and his death would not be known. I told him I would be happy to send a copy of the tape to his parents to let them know what had happened. He thought for a moment then said they wouldn't care. He could not think of anyone who would care; so, he went on to spirit with a friend who came to meet him. There is always someone there to help but the person coming over is sometimes too confused to respond to them.

Those souls who are confused, and have difficulty releasing their past associations with the earth plane, will need reassurance of their demise. This is especially true of those who die in a nursing home where they have been confined in one room for a long time. They mentally recreate the room and the daily routine they are accustomed to when they die, and they are usually angry because no one could hear them or help them.

A person who has spent many years in a house where they have had little contact with the outside world, will also recreate his home and previous routine. He will go about life as if he were still alive and will resent any intrusion into his home. If a new owner tries to move in, he will try to discourage him with all kinds of psychic disturbance. Many times I have been ordered out of a person's imaginary home but I have always been able to free the ghost from his memory. Sensitive people will detect this activity and will react according to their beliefs about ghosts or spirits.

The great majority of people who die will be met by loved ones who have come to meet them. The loved ones having been through the transition process will be able to help the newcomer become adjusted to the new experience. If there are no loved ones available, a person's guide will be there to help.

To assist in the transition process are many persons in the astral plane who are greeters. Also, there are healers who will help those souls who think they are still sick, to understand they no longer have a physical body that can be sick.

Some people who have strong preconceived ideas about death and do not believe in survival, may find themselves in a situation where they will need some outside help. If they believe that death is the end, and there is nothing more to come, they will find themselves in total darkness for that is their expectation. The guides in spirit will try to contact these souls in the darkness, to let them know there is a continuation of life in another dimension.

These souls, who are in denial, will often refuse to acknowledge the guides, because of suspicion or disbelief. Sometimes a person will adamantly refuse to accept the fact that he is dead, which, of course, is true. Accepting this truth would mean he would have to accept the fact of survival, and this is contrary to his beliefs. In some of these situations it is often easier for the guides to bring the soul to a rescue worker for counseling.

We have to recognize that the next level of consciousness is an energy field where our thoughts and desires are manifested as real. Once this is understood, it is easy to see how, at this next level of awareness, we create our own reality by the thoughts we think. The same is true on the earth plane, but here we are restricted by the time constraints of this dimension.

As the only things we can take into the next world are our character and our memory, we automatically go to the level of understanding that befits us.

Everyone has to outgrow his attachments and this includes attachment to people as well as material possessions. I could say, "Everybody goes to heaven," depending, of course, on what a person's idea of heaven happens to be.

It is in the realm of ideas that many people have difficulty letting go of the past. Many religious, political, and social differences make up an important part of our character and these associations seem difficult to relinquish. Many people appear in uniforms and other styles of clothing that have not been worn for hundreds of years.

I think that when a person returns to visit the earth plane, he automatically re-identifies with the image he had when he was here before. We are what we think we are; so, in the next plane we automatically recreate the being our memory recalls. I think the same applies in reverse. An Afro-American young man came through one day, very angry. He was cursing what he called "Whitey" because of some slight he had received.

When I tuned him to the light, he saw many white persons and said he wouldn't go there. I told him I had special powers and could make him white. Would he like that? There was silence for a while then he said, "No." So, I had him look around for someone from his family. He found his grandmother and went happily into spirit to join her. Deeply ingrained emotions are hard to relinquish.

I have had several runaway slaves and other Afro-Americans who have died at the hands of bigots. They cannot understand why they are attacked when they have done nothing wrong. Quite recently a man came through who was shackled in irons. He did not know his name, he did not know his parents, he did not know what year it was. He only knew he could not move because of the shackles. Apparently the slaves were secured at night, and he had died in the shackles. This was his primary thought when he died. He did not want to speak to me at first because the "Boss man" would whip him. When I got him to look at the light he could see some of the other slaves he had worked with in the fields, so I sent him to them.

Those who kill innocent people for racial or religious differences, who believe in this double standard, need a lot of help to overcome their guilt when they learn the truth. A feeling of superiority is the sign of an inferior person who has a lot to learn about the fact that we are of one life-force.

I find that people who have a good sense of who they are and have some knowledge of the fact of survival do not spend much time in the level known as the astral plane. They are ready to move on into the spirit world. A spiritualist will immediately look for some guide or loved one who has been communicating with him while he was on earth. As soon as a thought goes out for help, it is immediately answered. If a loved one is not readily available, then a guide will come forward and offer help.

No matter how angry or bitter a person is when they are on the earth plane, they quickly change when they recognize they have died and have been brought to me for help. It sometimes seems that most people have something to be upset about, and there are many who have great anger. As soon as I can, I get them to look at that light and their anger begins to dissipate. They are then very receptive to my suggestions for their anger is generally covering some fear or some guilt. They can all feel the warmth from the light embracing them, accepting them, urging them to come home to those loved ones who are waiting for them.

The light they see is not a place as we know a place on the earth plane. It is a radiation of love that is surrounding the guides and others who have preceded us. We all have a light radiating from our heart center, but the advanced souls have a brilliant light that is sometimes too bright and difficult for those in transition to accept. They have to learn to focus and, as they accept the love that comes from this light, they are accepting the fact of their death on earth and their transition to the spirit world.

Many people, when they are tuned into the light, will see it as a tunnel. They will be drawn into the tunnel, and feel the gentle pull as they are drawn along into the spirit world. This is also an experience a person may have when meditating, or in a near-death experience.

I have learned over the years that love is everywhere and is the basis of everything. It is as if we are born in a state of love and have been moving away from it, creating a world of make-believe. I believe we are all on our way back to this state of unconditional love. Eventually we will realize we already have this love within us.

We create our own problems by failing to acknowledge this love that is within us, waiting for expression. We must come eventually to accept the realization that whatever we do in life is our interpretation of this creative force of love. It is as if the creative essence is expressing itself through us and we determine our own reality.

In the next state of awareness, the astral or dream state, the experience is like in a dream. We exhibit a duplicate body which has similar sensory faculties to the physical body. These senses are more creative, and there is a different time order. This is the fourth dimension we have entered, and it takes time to get accustomed to it. As we take all our traits and characteristics with us, we quickly learn that life after this one is just a continuation, not a death or a change of identity.

Usually, it is not very difficult for the guides to make people realize they are no longer on the earth plane. There is a wonderful sense of peace that descends over them as they disengage from the earth, and this helps most people make the necessary change of perception. It is an inner peace that comes, and can only be known on earth during a deep mystical meditative experience.

There is a feeling of total surrender when this happens but we maintain our free will wherever we are, and no one can take that away from us. Because of this there are some who, when they die, think they are still alive on earth and will decide to reject those who come to help them. However, they can be influenced in the astral plane by a rescue worker as easily as they can be influenced on the earth plane. All the rescue worker needs is some feelings of compassion, and to let them know it is all right for them to go on into spirit.

Some trance mediums volunteer to help in the work and allow these souls in need to use the medium's auric atmosphere to get some counseling. The personal guide of these lost souls is able to influence them to come to the rescue worker. They do not usually refuse this contact because they believe they are speaking to someone on the earth plane. This, of course, is true and it confirms their belief that they are still alive on earth.

I have been doing this work for many years and have helped thousands of souls to free themselves from their mistaken beliefs. I would like to share some information I have gathered from some of the guides who work on this program.

One guide, named Brother Joseph, said he had volunteered to find people who need help and to influence them to come to the rescue workers for counseling. He told me that once they are rescued and accept the guide or relative, they are taken to different parts of the spirit world. They are taken to an area where they can work out their problems and attachment to the earth plane.

Often the attachment is for material things they have worked so hard to accumulate on earth and are loath to let them go. They are kept at the same level of vibration until they begin to look for something else; then, they go on to their loved ones. One woman refused to let me send her on as she had several fur coats and beautiful gowns. She had been told she could not take them into the spirit world. I told her I would lock them up and if she did not like the next world she could come back again.

Sometimes it is a sense of unfinished business or a feeling of responsibility for some project not completed that stops them from going on. I tell them that they will be able to see what is happening to their project from the next level and this usually satisfies them.

The sick are taken to a place where they learn that all sickness dies with the physical body and that the spirit body is perfect. When a person comes through to me in a rescue session, and tells me he is sick I can usually get him to change his self-concept and remove any ideas of sickness he thinks he still has.

It is sometimes difficult to get some of them to open up, especially those who have overdosed on drugs. They are in a euphoric state that they think are the effects of the drugs they have taken. They do not want to lose this feeling, and I have to convince them that the feeling they have is a spiritual one, free of drug influence. Usually they are looking for drugs or are protecting their stash and are suspicious of my intentions.

Fortunately, there are many souls in spirit who are working with people who are in transition, and I can call on them to help if necessary. The previous history of the one being helped is not relevant to the helpers from spirit. It seems they know that everyone is in transition to a higher life so why worry about the past. It seems there a sense of divine indifference to what has happened in the past.

I know that deep down everyone wants to go home to spirit when they leave this world. However, guilt is the one thing that will stop a person from progressing. Memory is both a positive and a negative thing, and unless we can recognize that all of life's experiences are there for us to learn, we will punish ourselves for our past.

When a rescue session is in progress, the room is brightly lit and there is no seance-like atmosphere. This whole process is by mental telepathy. The medium who has volunteered to do this work will probably not be aware of anything that has been happening. Mostly, they do not even want to hear the tapes of the sessions unless there is something of particular importance.

Some of the beings are in terrible distress when they come through. They need more help than those who have some guilt as a result of some minor infraction. Many hardened criminals would like to return to earth to put right what they have done, and some would like to return for revenge on someone who has offended them or killed them. When they discover they cannot return, some of them surround themselves with darkness. These are automatic candidates for rescue work.

The realization that there is no death comes as a terrible shock to those who thought they could do as they wish on earth and have no consequences in spirit. Although there is no judgment or punishment, when they learn that a confrontation with a previous victim is possible they will often try to hide. As on earth, each person has to live with who he is.

Recently, a young lady came through, and said she had been waiting a long time for help. I asked her what had happened, and she told me she had been cycling down a mountain trail and some man in a pick-up truck had edged her over the side. She said she was covered in bugs and would I get them off her. She must have been there quite some time and had died of exposure, unable to move. She said he was laughing as he did this to her. He will have a shock when he realizes there are consequences to such behavior.

We all do things we regret and hope to be forgiven for our lapses. If only we could change the past.

Sometimes a victim will have progressed to a level where he would like the guilty one to know everything is all right and that he is waiting to greet and help the offender. This sometimes has the desired result, and sometimes the grudges are too deeply embedded. This causes the reverse effect, and the guilty person will try to hide even though he can feel the love from the victim.

I have found that differences are resolved very quickly when people get to spirit. There is a reason for all things that happen on the earth plane. When a person hurts someone, then he realizes that anger and fear are self-destructive, he will try to make amends and apologize to the one he has hurt.

Racial and religious beliefs, and especially discrimination, are immediately seen as belonging only to the earth plane and are no longer relevant in the spirit world. For most people, these beliefs disappear when we get to the other side. However, some resentments can linger on for a while.

It is only natural that people on earth are concerned about relatives they have lost. I am sometimes asked to make a contact with someone in spirit, for a person who feels their loved one had no faith in God. I tell the person on earth the same as I tell a person being rescued who tells me they do not love God. I tell them that God loves them, so it's okay. If they are persistent, I will try to contact the person by using clairvoyance but not rescue work.

I feel that rescue work is the function of the guides in spirit, and if they feel that a contact is appropriate, it will happen. The selection process that decides who will be brought for rescue is beyond my control. The cases that are brought are usually souls in trouble and need special help. I have requested a contact for a very special situation but it is rare. I usually handle personal requests in my meditation groups. I feel the guides are in a better position than I am to handle situations of this kind.

I can remember on one occasion when I asked to speak to someone for a friend, they absolutely refused to come through and speak to me. The guide reminded me that everyone has free will at every level of our being, and I was left with the decision of what to tell my friend.

The transition to spirit is usually completely painless and very smooth. The fear of death has only the power that we give it. If it were possible for all people to realize that there is nothing but love and acceptance waiting for us in the next world, life on earth would be so much easier for everyone.

CHAPTER FOUR

RESCUE WORK EXAMPLES

THESE EXAMPLES OF ACTUAL CASES that have been dealt with over the years will give the reader an idea of the significance of this work. Many people cross over to spirit and have no idea what to expect. Different religiohs have various ideas of what is reality, especially where the next life is concerned, and there is generally confusion for most souls after the change called death.

A typical rescue work session lasts about thirty to forty minutes. The medium will go into trance and I will invite the first person to speak to me. The following is from a tape recorded at a session recently in my home.

JB: "Hello friend, come in and talk to me. My name is John, what's your name?"

Voice: "Frank."

JB: "Do you know where you are?"

Frank: "Yes I'm in the motel room, and I'm in trouble, I got caught. My wife saw me. I tried to hide."

JB: "What's the matter?"

Frank: "It's my wife. She's raging. She's waving a gun"

JB: "That's all over now. She shot you and you died."

Frank: "No, I'm in the room and I'm OK. But there's no way I can go home now."

JB: "There's no way you can go home for you are now in the spirit world. It's your memory that makes you think you are still in the motel room."

Frank: "Because I am. She was mad at me because I was laughing at her."

JB: She can't hear you now. If you try to talk to her she won't answer you. How old are you Frank?"

Frank: "Fifty-six and I'm in big trouble."

JB: "Well, you're not in big trouble really, You haven't yet accepted the fact that you were shot and killed. Look, Frank, I want you to look straight up ahead of you and you'll see a beautiful light shining down on you. Look into that light and tell me what you see."

Frank: "Wow, there's my mother. She died some time ago"

JB: "Do you see now that there is no death. She looks very much alive and so do you. Is she saying anything?"

Frank: "She just said, 'Won't you ever learn, come over here.'"

JB: "Go and join her now. She will show what to do."

Frank went off into spirit. Then there followed a typical stream of subjects, such as:

A forty-six year old woman named Karen who slipped and fell in her bathroom.

Janet who was rowing her boat and had a heat stroke. She thought she had to keep rowing.

Stacey, thirty-one-year-old drug overdose victim.

Cody, forty-three-year-old cowboy thrown from his horse and killed.

Jessica, fifty-six-year-old. Did not disclose how she died.

Simon, forty-three, waiting in hospital for a heart transplant operation.

End of session.

Many people become so attached to the earth plane that they have difficulty letting it go. In rescue work I have to try and change their thinking in some way, and I will resort to all kinds of stories to get them out of the darkness and into the light. Guides in spirit told me to use any means to get the soul to look into the light and then they will take over and help the person adjust to the new experience.

The light is a level of consciousness from which there is an outpouring of love. It is one of the higher levels of awareness to which we are compatible. The task of rescue work is to free the being from his fears, and get him to connect with this light. Then it becomes a battle of wits to get the person to accept the suggestions of the rescue worker.

The vibration of this light is more rapid than we experience on the earth plane, and it is part of the creative energy that is the basis of all things. We know this vibration as love and it is the area of existence which I refer to as the spirit world. Love is an emotion to us on the earth plane; however, it is really the creative essence of all that is in both the spirit and earth planes.

Rescue work is conducted on the astral plane, which is the level of awareness we all experience immediately after we die. The astral plane is the dream state or emotion/desire plane where we outgrow many of the attachments we have to the physical world.

The only tool the rescue worker has, is the use of suggestion and I have been able to cure blindness, AIDS, cancer, as well as any other sickness by changing the ideas of the person. I have given arms and legs to those that need them, because the astral plane is responsive to the ideas of the observer.

One man who had been blown to bits could see pieces of himself scattered around him. I told him I could reassemble him and proved it by a wave of my hand. I usually tell the person that it is their power that makes these changes, not me, for once free of the limitations of the earth plane we can manifest ourselves as we wish.

Despite the thousands of situations I have encountered in this work, I still have some strong emotional reactions to some of the tragedies that have befallen people as they make their transitions to spirit. I am well aware that all the problems from the earth plane will disappear once the deceased person has adjusted, but I cannot help being compassionate and concerned when a soul comes over in torment from mistreatment or abuse.

A woman came through once, crying and saying she could not understand what had happened. She said she was trying to reach her son who was swimming. She said she had jumped into the water after him because he had trouble. He said he was very tired and could not swim against the current. She said she kept reaching for him but could not quite make contact. I explained to her that she had drowned and I could pull her from the water. I tuned her into the light and she saw her son waiting for her there.

It is the little children who are victims of sodomy, incest, neglect or brutality that are the most tragic. These little children have no concept of death and are very confused with what has happened to them. They only know to cry out for their parents and are often scared to talk to me. They may have been told not to talk to strangers; so, if some strange adult has hurt them, they will try to hide. What is even more confusing for them is when their own parents have been the ones to hurt or abuse them. If those responsible for the cruelty could realize that there is no death and that children have a tremendous readjustment when they are released from the earth plane. Perhaps the abuser would think twice before they act out their anger or lust on an innocent child. For instance, one man came through sobbing. He kept saying, "She wouldn't stop crying." He had shaken his baby to death; then he had killed himself. Suicide often follows such incidents.

Of course we are all responsible for our actions and the offenders have to live with who they are. When they die and arrive in the astral plane and realize there is no death, they learn that they have to outgrow the conditions they have created for themselves. There is no judge waiting to send them to hell or mete out any punishment. They do a very good job of that on themselves.

The only hell is a personally created one. I have actually had people come through who are looking for hell, thinking that is what they deserve. One man came through who thought he was in the pit of hell. Whenever he tried to get out, hundreds of hands were pulling him back. I told him I could release him and simulated that I pulled him out. I told him he was now free. I asked him to help by telling all those in the pit that they could follow him into the light. He went on to those who were waiting for him, followed by a stream of others who had witnessed his release.

When I began this work, I was surprised at the wonderful organization in the spirit world as everyone going to spirit has available to them all the help they need. Unfortunately, some of the hardened criminals are difficult to convince that there is another way open for them to outgrow the past. Their anger is like a barrier around them and they do not want to hear about love and a new life.

There is special help where the children are concerned. There is a beautiful, angelic looking Nun who is surrounded by light and who is always available when I send over children. Her name is Sister Mary. When the children see her, they all say how pretty she is and often ask if she is an angel.

Although Sister Mary is the one who always comes for the children, she has told me that there are hundreds of helpers for the children in spirit.

The most surprising thing for me is the fact that when she comes to help a four-year-old, she will be surrounded by several four-year-old children. If the child is a teenager, she will have teenagers with her. This helps the children because I am able to tell them that they can play with these other children until their relatives or friends come to join them. Because of time differences this will seem to be very soon.

In some situations I can show the person being rescued the victim who has been hurt by his behavior. The victim may be waiting for the one who hurt him, not out of revenge but with love and forgiveness. It is remarkable how things are resolved in the spirit world. The beauty, love, and understanding that comes from the higher spirits brings forgiveness for the past misdeeds of others. Sometimes, when the guilty person is confronted by a victim he may have difficulty accepting the situation. The guilty one will first deny any involvement; then, he will admit to what he has done and then may go to the one who is waiting for him. Sometimes, the sense of guilt is so strong he will still refuse to admit his involvement. In cases like this I send them to someone else in spirit, such as a relative or guide who can help them.

The speed of the personality change is amazing. As we leave the earth plane the years seem to drop away and we begin to forget much of the experience of this life. Our memory is kind to us and the past becomes like a dream, similar to the past in this life. It seems our total being is enriched by the various experiences of the earth plane; however, the details are soon outgrown.

I was told many years ago when I started this work that I should not play God and judge people. I was only to get them to open up and tell me what their problems were, to help them to resolve them, to realize where they are, and send them on to the light. As soon as they open up and look at the light, they see the guides or relatives waiting for them and there is an immediate personality change. The guides then take over, and my work is finished.

This has always been the case. No matter how angry or bitter a person is when he is brought to the worker, as soon as he looks at that light the anger dissipates and he is quieter and quickly receptive to suggestions. He will feel the love and warmth embracing him, accepting him, urging him to come home to those who are waiting.

Love is present at every level of consciousness and is there for us to use, or abuse. The light I tune people into is the radiation of love that is surrounding the guides. We all have light around us, radiating from our heart center, but the advanced guides have a brilliant light that is sometimes too difficult for those in transition to handle. They have to learn to focus, and as they adjust to the light they are accepting the fact that they have died, and are in transition to a new life.

I have learned over the years that love is everywhere. It is as if we are born in a state of love and have been moving away from it, while waiting to come back to this state of pure, unconditional love. We must come to the realization that whatever we do in life is our interpretation of this creative force of love. It is as if the creative force of the universe is expressing itself through us. While on this earth plane, we are the representatives of this divine force, literally God in manifestation.

We create our own problems by failing to acknowledge the love that is within us, waiting for expression. It is as if there is a force within us that is constantly driving us foreword to seek new experiences, but it is also quietly calling us home and reminding us of our divine heritage.

Not all rescue cases are tragic. There are a few that are extremely funny.

For example, one situation I love to relate was about a man in a nursing home. When I contacted him he said he was in a lot of trouble as he couldn't move. I assured him he could and that he could get out of the bed whenever he liked, which he did. When I tuned him into the light, he said, "Oh God, I thought I was in trouble before. I was married eight times and there are seven of them up there looking at me. What do I do now?" I said to him, "What do you think they've been talking about up there? Go and enjoy the reunion." He said, "I was always good to them; there was always plenty of money." I told him that they would not be there if they didn't want to be. All he had to do was to go over to them and all would be resolved. I would love to know the outcome of the meeting.

In another situation, there was a bank robber who did not realize he had been killed by the police and he was holed up in a cabin with bags of money. At first he thought I had come to steal his money and resisted my intrusion. Then, he thought I was from the police. After I made him aware of his situation and explained that money was useless in the next world, he wanted to give me the money!!

There have been a few cases where a man will draw out all his money and bury it somewhere where his wife could not get it. Once I tried to get one of them to tell me who he was, and where he lived, so that I could send a copy of a tape to his wife, but he didn't trust me. The thought of lots of money rotting under a rose bush in his garden! What a waste, and what a thing to do to someone who has had to put up with her husband's illness and demise. I hope she found it.

Money, apart from the bank robbers, is one of the big problems people have in letting go of the earth plane. One man was extremely angry because the family was not using his money as he thought they should. I told him the money was left to them to use as they liked, and he had best forget about the money and change his perception and look to the light. He did not like to hear that but he eventually understood and went into spirit.

It is true that you can only take your memory and your character with you into the next world. Many people find they can recreate material things by thought. When they become aware of their surroundings in the next plane of consciousness they will make beautiful clothes and cars, furniture and jewelry and will try to protect them from intruders like me.

One man surrounded his hiding place with a pit of snakes and was amazed that I could get in. I told him the snakes were in his imagination, not mine. Some people are quite creative in their choice of defence; mostly, they project their own fears.

Another man recreated his bright red pick-up and was very proud of it. I tried to explain to him that it was an illusion but he wouldn't listen. I told him I would change it to a gold color and I made that happen. He was very angry; so, I changed it back. When I did that, he could see that the truck was in his imagination and he was ready to listen to the truth and move on. A man came through roaring like a lion. He thought he was keeping a number of children away from his property. He imagined that they would run away whenever he roared, which they did. I had to explain to him that he was creating this whole scenario and that he could keep on doing this forever if he wished. Otherwise, he could change his attitude and the children would go away and he could go on.

One day during a regular sitting the medium was surrounded by a beautiful light. A soft-spoken voice identified itself as a nun who had sinned and become pregnant and committed suicide. This meant she had a triple burden:

pregnancy, suicide, and the baby's death. She wanted confession, punishment, and absolution so I sent her on to Father Ralph to take care of her.

In contrast to the nun, a man named Sam came through. He was a hit-man for the mob. He died in the electric chair, and he couldn't understand how he had not died. I told him that he was not dead as he was speaking to me, and the people he thought he had killed were all alive in the spirit world.

Sam told me he had killed hundreds of people over the years, but I think he was exaggerating. When I tuned him in he saw a crowd of people he had killed. He asked, "Is it all right to go there?" I told him he could go and confront them or he could go to some family members who were there.

He didn't think he deserved much, and I had to reassure him that he had a different understanding of life when he did what he did back in the days of prohibition.

The image creating ability of the mind makes all things possible in the next state of awareness. It is the people who on earth had little or nothing, find they can fulfill their desires at this time, and outgrow their need for material things. Many of them need a nudge to let go of these material things and I sometimes tell them I will protect their goods while they go to the light to talk to someone they know. This ploy seems to work as I don't think anyone would come back to the loneliness of a make believe life in the astral plane.

When people hang on to their material possessions and keep other people away, they are enforcing loneliness upon themselves. I used to tell people that they would have no one to share their things with but that didn't work, they were too defensive. Often when I remind souls of this truth, they realize that the company of family and friends is more important than material things and they will go on into the light.

Organized religion creates a lot of problems for the rescue worker. In the Catholic faith people who die without absolution or final rites are told they will go to purgatory. There is no such place. When they come through and say they are in that state, I quickly get them to see the truth and send them on. If they do not accept what I say, there is a Father Ralph in the spirit world who will satisfy whatever they think they need. Many Catholics who die in air crashes or in isolation cannot receive last rites. However, Father Ralph can take care of them.

In some religions they teach that everyone goes to sleep until they are awakened by Jesus. On one occasion, I was in one of these supposed dormitories and was told to be quiet. I quickly made them all wake up and told them I was a messenger from the Lord and they were to go to the light to meet him. It worked beautifully.

Some ministers tell their flock that they must wait with them in the afterlife until they are allowed to go to heaven. Sometimes, hundreds of people are waiting with their leader.

On several occasions the following dialogue has taken place:

Minister: "Have you come to be saved?" (in a loud voice)

Me: "No, I have come to save you. I am a messenger from the Lord and I would like to address your flock and tell them to tune into the light and go to their loved ones there above you. There is no need for you all to stay here."

Minister to his flock: "Don't listen to him. He is a heathen."

Some of the people have heard my message and will start going over to meet their loved ones. The minister will start screaming at his people and at me, but I will eventually calm him down and get him to see the error of his ways. One minister after he realized his error said, "Oh God, what have I done?" I quickly helped him to see that he had acted in good faith.

I now use a different approach. I now compliment them on the fine work they have done for the Lord and suggest they should lead their people to the greater life in the light. One man unfortunately saw a lot of people in the light that he thought were sinners and did not want to go there. This refusal is rare as deep down everyone wants to go home to spirit, but some ministers like to maintain control over their flock.

Another problem is the attitude of family members on the earth plane toward a son whose sexual preference is different from the norm. Many people with AIDS, having no contact with family, die in isolation. Fortunately, there are workers in spirit who are free of prejudice and will work with this group. One man in particular is called Doctor Bill. He was a doctor in an AIDS hospital in San Francisco who contracted the disease himself.

He came and spoke to me one day from spirit, and he asked me if I would be willing to work with him and his patients. We have worked together ever since. Mostly the victims know him but if I have any difficulty getting the person to open up, he will come.

Another great worker for these victims is a nurse who also contracted this disease from a hypodermic needle which accidently pierced her skin. These wonderful workers are still helping the unfortunate victims.

Many AIDS victims imagine they are still in the hospital ward; so, my job is to convince them that they have died and that Doctor Bill is there to help them. Sometimes a relative who has been in spirit for awhile and has outgrown his prejudices will appear and greet the person.

When a person approaches the earth plane vibration again he will exhibit the idea he has of himself from the past. Dr. Bill and the nurse both appear in their uniforms so the patients think they are still in hospital. But it is not too difficult for me to get them to see the true situation.

The psychological damage and the deep depression the AIDS victim feels as a result of family rejection makes it difficult sometimes to get the person to accept help. I often get the feeling they have welcomed death because of the nature of their disease, and the lack of response to the love they had for their family.

Sometimes they will tell me to keep away or I will get infected. They know they have a terminal illness and the feeling of despair is evident in their voices. It is a great feeling helping them get free.

One surprise for me is the dedication of some of the doctors and nurses who do not want to leave their patients. They are still helping people in the astral plane as if they were still working on the earth plane.

Our prejudices quickly change when in spirit. We learn that all people are equal, and a person can show himself in whatever form he wishes. There is a reason for all things, and there is a grand design to life. Our beliefs on earth are not necessarily true. We learn that goodness is what we approve of and evil is what we disapprove of. In the final analysis we create our own value system of right and wrong.

Death is nothing to fear. There are some problems for people who have had long illnesses, but the problems disappear as soon as the transition is begun. Physical things stay on the earth plane, and spirits biggest task is getting people to let go of the attachments. Unfortunately, the next plane allows our memory to recreate them.

It seems we take not only our memory and character with us when we die, but also we take some of our supposed problems too. This ability to reproduce the past often creates problems for some people as it tends to retard a person's progress until he or she outgrows this attachment.

One situation I had was with a woman who said she couldn't get up as she weighed six hundred pounds. I told her I had special powers and, if she gave me her hand, I could help her out of her body. I simulated the motions of pulling her up and she became free. I told her to leave the body behind and go on to her loved ones. At first she had difficulty understanding how she could be free and still see her body. Eventually, she was happy to accept the new situation and she went on to the spirit world as a slimmer version of herself.

Another situation which demonstrates the power of suggestion occurred during an out-of-body experience. I was taken to a room where there were several people standing around a woman who was on her hands and knees. She had adopted the head of a cat and was making cat noises. For some unknown reason I grabbed her by the scruff of the neck and shook her, and said "Stop this nonsense, you are a beautiful person." She stood up as a beautiful woman and I was returned to my physical body.

Remember, we create our own reality by the thoughts we think. It is better to raise our thoughts and outgrow these attachments while on the earth plane than to wait for the next world.

I believe that when we leave this plane, it is like sailing away from a place that has been one of learning and growth. We live through a wide range of emotional experiences which causes us to redefine who we are as we go through life towards the end result which is progress.

It is given to few people to be free of fear of the unknown. We are carefully trained to believe a lot of nonsense in order to control our natural instincts and to create a fear of the life after death, but we quickly outgrow that fear in the spirit world. One of the first things we learn is that fear has only the power that we give it. Unfortunately, many religions use fear as a control of their followers.

One case showing the power of fear occurred about five years ago. A young boy came through complaining how he hated the stuffy crowded place where he was. He was in a hut at a prison camp in World War II. The children were told that they would be shot if they tried to leave the hut; so, they stayed there. After they had been gassed, they could see their parents in spirit who were calling them; however, they were afraid to go to them. I gave him permission to go to his parents and the rest soon followed.

During a regular meditation session, I was leading the group in raising its consciousness to a higher level when a child's voice came through one of the rescue mediums. An eight-year-old girl said she and many other children were trapped behind bars for being naughty. I asked her who put her there, and she said her parents had told her that she would go to jail if she played in the street. She had been killed in the street by a car, and she had imprisoned herself when she went to the astral plane.

She said, "My daddy won't even look at me or speak to me." I explained to her that her daddy could not see her, but I could help her and the others. I told her to look to the light and when I removed the bars they should all go to the relatives who would be there to help them. I removed the bars, and it was like a flood of children racing to meet their loved ones or the guides who were waiting for them.

Parents should avoid using fear as a discipline for children. Children in their formative years are very impressionable and believe their parents, even when they appear not to. Remember children are testing reality to find their own identity.

One case showing the effect of parents' behavior even after the death of a child is clearly illustrated in the following.

A child said, "I was in the hospital and I was sick. It was awful. My mother didn't know how sick I was; she thought I had the flu. I didn't have the flu; I had something of the intestine. My mother cried and cried, and my father doesn't like her anymore; he goes away and leaves her. He says she killed me. I tried to tell him. I couldn't get anyone to listen. No one can hear me."

I told her I could hear her. She told me her name was Audrey and she was ten. She lived in Portland, Oregon, and she was very upset. She continued, "My mum is all alone now. Can you tell my daddy it was not her fault? He goes away and leaves her. She loves me and wants to keep me. She thinks she didn't take care of me. Tell my daddy it was not her fault. He hates her and she is very lonely."

Audrey had spent many earth years worrying about her parents. I sent her on to Sister Mary so that she could reach another level of understanding. She had attached herself to the earth plane consciousness and could not understand why no one would speak to her.

I later attempted to recall her for more information but she had gone on into spirit. From the incidents she had described, it is obvious that many earth years had passed, and it would not help to interfere with the outcome of her parents' problems.

I have been told by guides from spirit that learning continues in the astral plane and the spirit world. Apparently it is a process of outgrowing attachments, of letting go of the encumbrances that clutter our lives. We can be trapped by our beliefs just as easily as we are by the material things we want to hang on to.

Sometimes a minister will say he never thought it would be so easy to make the transition. The truth is so simple that smothering it in ritual and rhetoric creates confusion, even for priests and ministers.

Death is not a curse; rather, it is a promotion to spirit. I wish everyone could experience the tremendous spiritual upsurge that comes to those who are freed of this earthly vale of tears. Transition from level to level is achieved by spiritual growth, not by what or who we think we are. Many a poor worker is welcomed into the light because of the kindness and service to others they have shown in their life and many wealthy persons find they have a lot to learn about human relations.

CHAPTER FIVE

BECOMING A PERSON

WHEN WE ARE BORN INTO THIS DIMENSION, we interact with our environment and are influenced by the people and things around us. We immediately begin to form a system of beliefs as to what is reality. We have automatic reactions to all the sensations that we feel and each sensation is given a specific meaning. These meanings that we apply to life differ from person to person, from day to day, and from hour to hour. What really matters to an individual is the specific meaning of a person's life at any given moment.

Each day as we awaken we become aware of our surroundings, and we immediately recall who we are based on our beliefs about ourselves. It is our memory which affirms our identity in this physical world, and we create a personality as a result of the thoughts we think.

These thoughts are the result of a combination of factors which include our genetic heritage, the cultural conditioning, the environment, and our behavior. Or, we are what we do, with what we are born with, and in whatever situation we find ourselves. Our character is molded by internal and external influences, and it is the source of the internal influences that we try to identify in our search for the truth about ourselves. Somehow we know there is a higher force that creates all that is, and there is a purpose and grand design to this life. We have to accept this on faith until we can raise our thoughts to a higher level of perception and see for ourselves.

We seem always to have the "Who am I" question open before us as if it is unanswerable. We pursue answers to this question in religion and science, and we are constantly faced with accepting the choice of either faith or logic.

I have found that blind faith is an excuse to stop searching because we accept the idea that some supreme force will take care of everything for us. Whereas logic tends to be materialistic in its attempt to deny belief in favor of scientific knowledge. The scientific method does not apply when we are investigating such things as Spiritualism because the phenomenon of mediumship cannot be measured and is not repeatable on demand.

Evidence of survival of the human personality after death can often be verified by sitters after a meeting with a medium.

The fact is, there are people who have extrasensory perception and other psychic abilities, and there is intuition and inspiration that comes to us from sources other than logic. Many people have had moments of extended sensitivity where they have been able to foresee events in the future, predictive dreams are common, and some houses are haunted.

My studies into both approaches to truth have encouraged me to look within and I have found that the "I AM" is really the only thing I can be sure of. The "I AM" is that part of a person's being that identifies with the environment. It precedes every thought of self in this physical state of awareness, and is the link with the spiritual aspect of man. It functions through the ego and identifies with the third dimension.

Everything outside of the self requires a belief, whether it is in science or some faith which is without the foundation of fact, as determined by the physical sciences.

I would like to share with you a meditation experience you might like to explore. I once reached a point of awareness in deep meditation in which I was in an area of pure energy which I assumed was the creative essence of all substance. There was a feeling of pure unconditional love and I had an intense desire to express this feeling and share it with others.

I found myself being drawn into different experiences so that as I returned to the physical plane there was a review of the many facets of my personality; so, I could look at myself becoming who I am at this time in my life. It was as if I were rapidly changing my sense of beingness at each level of realization that I passed through. It was as if I were gathering a script to be played out later.

If you would like to try this, after introspection to the inner self through meditation, assume you are a point of pure consciousness in the highest echelons of the spirit world and you have decided to pay a visit to the third dimension.

On the way to this world you will be aware of changes in the vibration rate of the self. As the vibration rate decreases, various levels of consciousness will be experienced and you will find you are compatible with each level. Each level is peopled by souls who are in the process of changing from one level to another. Time seems to slow down and the atmosphere appears to get denser as you proceed with your quest to explore the third dimension. You will gather some traits and characteristics that will provide a framework for the character you will become.

There is considerable preparation before you take the plunge into this world. The reason or purpose of your life to be will determine many of the conditions you will find after you are born. Without these purposes there would not be anything to keep you in this physical dimension. Once these purposes are fulfilled there may be a return to spirit. This may account for the seeming waste of a good person who dies at a young age, or the death of a newborn baby who lightly touches the earth and then returns to grow up in spirit form.

Remember, you are starting your journey from the highest levels of consciousness and you will have tremendous power within you. You will be covering or screening these higher powers as you pass through each level of awareness. Each level of consciousness from the center outward has a lesser vibration rate and the power is reduced. The powers of the higher levels are too strong for this dimension and we as human beings could not accommodate them.

Assuming you have lived on the earth before, there will be past memory associations to help decide on the forthcoming experiences. There will have been an agreement with your parents and others who will play a significant role in the life to come. There will be a person who is quite evolved, whom you have known for a long time in other levels of awareness. He or she has agreed to be your guide and mentor for this excursion.

In the beginning this divine spark of life, your higher self, goes through this preliminary process, then enters a period of forgetting, or disassociating, from the spirit world to give you a fresh outlook. It is as if a veil is drawn between the earth plane and the spirit world. The veil is essential, for without it we would all be in spirit and there would not be any reason for the earth plane experience.

The moment this spark of life enters this world it sets up a defence barrier between itself and the world around it. No one can penetrate this barrier. It is very strong and we never let anyone close to us without our permission. No unwelcome entities can possess us for we are inviolate.

There are many cases of obsession, where a person has assumed other identities because they cannot deal with the life situation they are in. This is a self-defence mechanism which requires professional psychological help if it is a problem.

Our free will permits us to play any mind games we wish and we can assume any role that gives us a feeling of security. Unfortunately it also allows wild excursions of imagination with unusual results. The worship of show business idols or sports figures are examples of this.

In rescue work I see this demonstrated often. Many souls, realizing they have the power to create whatever surroundings they wish, will let their emotions and desires run wild. They may make claims to past identities from the devil to Jesus. Many souls want to come and save us from our sins.

One of the first entities I encountered was a man who said he was Judas Iscariot. I said to him that Judas had incarnated several times since the time of Jesus, why not use one of those identities. Seeing I was not about to fall for his game of trying to impress me he quickly left.

From a physical point of view, we have within us a central contact with all the other levels of awareness. If the teachings of the great masters are correct, that the "Kingdom of heaven is within us," then we must have access to all the inner planes. We can access these higher planes through the "I AM," which is the basis of our identity. It is the "I AM" that precedes every thought, feeling, or action we make in this life.

Around this initial barrier between the planes of awareness we create our self-concept, consisting of all the ideas we have about ourselves and have developed since our birth. We learn to adopt the role to suit the situation we are in; then we behave according to how we think we should behave, or choose to behave.

All these identities are preceded by the designation "I AM," and a simple computation of probability will show how there are limitless number of variations possible. This is how it is that we are totally unique, there is no one exactly like us.

Through our self-concept, we project our personality, the self-image, we think the world expects to see. We look out through this self-image as if it were a screen that protects the inner self. Which it does, very effectively.

At each moment of our lives we are limited by the experiences we have had, and there is no other way we can view the world except through this screen. We observe, evaluate, then act according to the value we place on the experience. This creates what we think is real for us in this dimension.

We wear this veneer of personality which we show the world and which has little to do with the real, higher self. When we meet another person, we exchange introductions and if it is agreeable to both parties, some information and feelings may be exchanged about who we are at deeper levels. If we feel we may not like the person we have met we will move away from the situation. These are the games we play when meeting someone.

The attempt to find stability in this world sometimes causes feelings of insecurity. Fortunately, the self is adaptable and we are able to constantly redefine ourselves to keep pace with the demands for change in this environment. However, too many changes in life will bring stress which I feel is the basis of many illnesses.

When we have problems in this life, it means we have lost sight of our divine heritage. Our attention is totally outer directed and we may call on the services of some

higher power for help. Whenever we raise our consciousness to a higher source a response will be forthcoming.
Unfortunately, we sometimes ignore, or don't allow, the
response to come through to us. We rarely trust anything
we cannot see or touch.

If we go to a counselor for help, he will try to adjust our
self-image to conform to socially acceptable standards. If
we ask a mystic, he will explain that the world is an idea in
our mind and we play games with it all the time. He may
point out that our self-concept is merely a set of ideas we
have about ourselves which are constantly changing. He
may also show how the "I am" is the closest we can get to
the true reality.

The medical doctor deals with the physical body, the
counselor deals with the emotions or intellectual levels of
activity, and the mystic deals with the first or ultimate
source of life.

This whole process can be viewed and experienced
through meditation. When we withdraw our attention
from the physical, emotional, and mental levels of consciousness, we can enter into states where we can see how
it all is. We can enter states where the oneness of all things
can be experienced, and we can observe the process of
creation taking place.

All the screens can be bypassed when we are able to raise
our consciousness to a higher level of awareness. Sometimes, it is possible to have this experience spontaneously,
as in the experience known as the descent of grace. It is as
if we are transported to a spiritual level of experience and
our perception of things changes. What has really happened is that we have opened ourself to a channel which
gives access to the astral plane and we have become temporarily aware of our own higher self.

Most people have experienced moments of intense
emotion. A person can be so deeply involved in an activity,

that there is a feeling of complete surrender to the moment and waves of ecstacy may sweep over the body.

Many people who feel they have suddenly found Jesus or the Lord, have experienced this moment of union with their true self. It has the ability to transform a person's life forever, it has such a profound affect upon a person that he feels he must share it with someone. The "Born Again Christians" or the Hare Krishna groups are good examples of this attitude.

Another example of consciousness raising would be when a person has a sudden traumatic experience, such as the loss of a loved one. The world becomes a place where he can no longer cope and he withdraws into another level of beingness. A gap appears in his protective screens and he becomes very vulnerable. He has lost some of the identities that have given him the stability which he used to stay attached to this world, and he needs to be healed by someone who understands his loss.

A student of mine once had a serious car accident which totalled her vehicle. She walked away completely un-harmed; however, from that moment, for about seven days, she had psychic awareness and could see auras around people. She felt only love toward everyone and saw only love emanating from them. She was pleased to return to normal awareness as she found the increased sensitivity disturbing. It seems we need our defenses in this dimen-sion, for this is the life we are concerned with now.

This visit to the third dimension will terminate eventu-ally as determined by the plan we have made before coming here. We take the memory and information with us to the next state of awareness and it becomes part of our total being, ready for our next experience.

The physical world and the astral planes are closely inter-active. We can switch easily from one to the other when we sleep and when we die. Once beyond these levels of experience the earth plane becomes a memory for a while and then is disregarded.

We experience this third dimension, and adopt beliefs about ourselves. We carry these ideas into the fourth dimension and express ourselves there as if we can apply this earthly frame of reference to the new experience. It doesn't always fit.

Depending on the intensity of the imprint of the beliefs about ourselves when we go to spirit we may be attracted to return to this state of awareness and go through a reincarnation experience and live in this world again.

The experiences of both the earth and astral planes are strictly associated with beliefs about ourselves, and it is only when we are able to let them go, that we can experience higher states of consciousness.

Many theories of reincarnation abound in this world, but the realization that we create time so that we can experience this dimension will help people understand. In seeking the higher states of awareness we bypass these earth-related concepts. Reincarnation, Karma, Astrology and other similar beliefs are not valid beyond the earth and astral planes.

In the Eastern religions the great desire is to break free of the "Wheel of Rebirth" and enter states of beingness known as Samahdi and Satori. These states are the first step to the awareness of the oneness of all things. That which we in the western world call the God force.

It is very difficult for us to realize that everything that is, was, or ever shall be, was created in an instant. We are a facet of this creative essence, and, as we create the time appropriate to the dimension we are experiencing, we only see the third dimension while we are in this state of awareness.

This planet is brought into being by the combined thoughts of all the people experiencing it, and we become co-creators by being attracted here.

By a wild stretch of imagination, the combined thoughts of mankind could destroy us through proliferation of destructive bombs or biological accidents. If such a thing happened, we would immediately recreate a world in another dimension.

There is no death. There is never a time when we are not conscious at some level or another.

CHAPTER SIX

PERSONAL BELIEFS

F ROM THE MOMENT WE ARRIVE IN THIS WORLD we interact
with the environment to the best of our ability, and we
immediately begin to form beliefs about the nature of this
reality. As we proceed along our path, we adopt and
outgrow many beliefs such as the Tooth Fairy and Santa
Claus. It is the beliefs we adopt that help shape the
character we portray to the world.

It is necessary for us to have a belief system or we would
not be able to remain in this state of awareness; we would
all be in the spirit world. We must have the belief that we
are alive and that we have a base in this third dimension to
which we can return. When we leave this state of consciousness in sleep or other forms of disorientation, the world
ceases to exist. Of course, we are still physically alive during
these absences. The subconscious mind has taken over the
task of maintaining life in this world while our self-image,
or astral body, is exploring the dream state or some other
level of awareness.

The physical sciences tell us we are living in a universe
of energy particles and our beliefs about the reality of the
world are erroneous. Apparently, we are a mass of energy
vibrating at thirty-three vibrations per second. So, as the

world around us is vibrating at the same rate, we see the world as a steady, objective phenomena.

Any distortion of this relationship between the self and other states will result in a loss of consciousness. If you have ever fainted or passed out from an anesthetic, you will know how unstable the world can be. Of course, it is our perception that changes as the world is always there for us when we return to this level of consciousness.

We must have some form of attachment to this earth plane at all times, even when we sleep. Mystics, tell us there is a silver cord of light particles through which we maintain a life-contact with the earth plane and through which we can return here when we awaken. That cord is indestructible. It cannot be severed or damaged in any way.

Beliefs can be very powerful. Many people believe that the planets and stars exert an influence on our daily lives. They will accept, or construct, complicated formulas and see relationships between the position of the planets and their future lives. It is at best an interesting diversion and is probably harmless. I have found that there are no planets or stars in the dream state or in any of the other levels of consciousness. They can be created mentally on the astral plane but they would have to be dreamed up.

The medical doctor uses beliefs in the power of the placebo. We treat the doctor as an exceptional person because of his degrees and believe he has the power of healing. The power of suggestion, or the reassurance by a doctor, has a lot to do with the healing process.

I believe that the greatest value of the extensive training a doctor has received is the accurate diagnosis of conditions in the physical body. Too many people believe false claims of wonder cures advertized in the media.

It is refreshing that many doctors are now open to consideration of alternative medicine and other methods of healing. Some of these methods, such as hypnosis, depend on beliefs or suggestion.

Religion is one of the strongest belief systems. The many varieties of religious experience that different people have had, form the basis of hundreds of faiths. Each religion is another attempt to describe reality and is based on an interpretation of the source from which their beliefs originate. There are many comforts to be found in the belief or faith that there is a divine power that looks after all things.

We hypothesize that what we see is reality. How can it be otherwise? We can easily forget that when we hear a tune, the ear hears one note at a time, and it is the memory of past experience and an expectation of future notes that allows us to hear a tune. Why are we surprised when we hear a wrong note? Who says it is a wrong note? It is a note like any other, but it just did not meet our expectation of what we remember we had heard before.

The same is true of the world at large. We learn the way things are supposed to behave and if they don't, there's something wrong. We create habit patterns in our minds which are the basis of our security and our automatic response mechanism to stimulus from outside. These habits allow us to walk and speak without thinking of every syllable we wish to say.

In rescue work I can change a person's belief in what he is seeing. A dead person trapped in a car, believing he is still in the car, will leave the vehicle as soon as I can convince him that he is able to. I have often told people that I will lift their car, or tree, or whatever they are trapped by and free them. They never question how I can lift thousands of pounds; they just come out of the situation. Then they are free to go on to the next set of beliefs they will adopt.

One man was trapped under the wheel of his wagon for over a hundred of earth time years. He said, "My stupid mule is over there eating grass and I can't get it to pull the wagon away." I soon lifted up the wagon and freed him. He was amazed at the amount of earth time that had passed since his accident. He thought it had been a few days.

At first it was difficult for me to understand how a person could be trapped for hundreds of years. Then one of the guides explained there are different times in the various planes of awareness. He reminded me that in a dream I could take a trip that on earth would take months; then, I could wake up and find I had only been asleep for a few minutes.

Apparently, time is related to the rate of vibration at each different level of awareness. I notice that in meditation and in dreams there is a change in the speed of everything around me.

In all out-of-body activities there seems to be time variations, and on the earth plane our appreciation of time varies according to our attitudes.

In some of the lower planes I have visited, time and everything else seems much slower and the atmosphere appears heavier and darker. The only light seems to come from the solar plexus area of the body and doesn't project very far. It makes the statement of Jesus that "The I AM is the light of the world," very plausible. In the higher planes we all radiate very strong and powerful lights, and the "Darker" worlds are very well named.

Another case involving time was a man who said he lived in the fifteen hundreds. He believed could not go to heaven because he was the illegitimate son of a woman who had not been allowed in the church to have him christened. She had been banished from the church and ostracized in society because she had sinned. He said he had no name and could not be buried in a church cemetery and was told by the minister that he would go to hell. He told me the name of his father was Tom. I told him I was a minister and would be happy to christen him. I told him his name would be Tomson, Son of Tom. He was thrilled. I gave him a blessing and off he went into the light.

The guides have told me to use any ploy to get the people to look into the light. Once they do, they immediately realize they have been looking in the wrong direction. Their attention had been directed toward the life they had left behind, and I have to redirect their thinking. As soon as they are able to make a contact with those who are waiting for them, they go off to join them. Only on rare occasions has anyone ever returned to speak to me. As people move away from the earth plane they begin to lose interest in this world very quickly.

When I am asked what happens when we die, or when I am in the company of a terminally ill person, I tell him that when he dies he should look up, or straight out ahead when he is free of the body; then he will see a beautiful light. If he will focus on that light he will see his loved ones.

There is nothing we have to do when in the astral plane to make contact with others around us. If we wish to join with a particular person, we have only to think of ourselves with the person and we are automatically drawn to them.

One man told me he was trapped in a tunnel cave-in and his body had been crushed. I told him I would pull him out of the mine but he thought it would be impossible. He obviously could not understand how this could be; how he could speak to me and how he could be dead at the same time. I explained that there is no death and I told him I had special powers and could free him. I just waved my hand over him, told him it was done, and to him it was.

These seemingly magical feats are performed by the persons themselves. I am only the catalyst helping them to do what they could do, if only they understood that they were creating their own reality.

The knowledge that we create our own reality should not be a problem for us. Too long man has thought of the world as being a stable thing, but modern science has changed all that. We now know we live in a field of energy and we are part of the creative process. It is in the dream world that we begin to realize that we do have the power to change our environment by thought.

People who have drowned and think they are still under water do not question how they can carry on a conversation with me. It seems we are where our attention is directed at any particular moment, and once free of the body our sense of reality changes.

One day a man came through who was a passenger on a ferry which capsized in the Aegean Sea. He said there were hundreds of people in the water. I convinced him he could walk on the water and asked him to lead the others to safety. He found he could walk on the water and gathered many of the others together and led them away to the light.

I often enlist the help of one person out of a group to help others to the light. In an aircraft that had run into a mountain at night, one person was able to free all the other passengers. They mostly were still sleeping, unaware that they were dead. It is the victim of sudden, unexpected death who thinks that he is still alive on earth. Many souls who have been killed in an accident will continue to do exactly what they were doing before.

When a rocket exploded after take-off over Florida I asked one of the guides what had happened to the crew. He told me that all but two of them knew immediately that they had been killed. The other two were allowed to continue their flight until they realized the others were not responding to them, then they raised the question of what had happened and that was the cue for them to come to realization of the disaster and the guides to step in.

Many times I have directed a soul to look into the light and he will see someone there waiting for him. I will then ask him to help me by rousing others from whatever condition they are in, so that he can lead them to the light also. This is especially true of an officer in charge of a group of men who had all been killed. When they were brought to me to be rescued, they were hiding in caves or dugouts and wanted me to be quiet. They thought they were still hiding from the enemy. I tried to explain that the war had been over for many years, and that was hard for them to accept.

In situations like this I know the men will obey the officer's orders as they have been trained to do in the past. So it is to the officer that I speak, knowing the men will follow him when I can convince him to accept the fact that he is dead.

The time differential makes it possible for people in the Civil War, both World Wars, Korean and Vietnamese conflicts to still believe they are alive and fighting the enemy. They are really surprised when they tune into spirit and see their parents waiting for them.

I would like any reader of this material to look at their own beliefs and see if there are any negative beliefs such as discrimination, anger or fear of others. It is better to work these things out in this world than to wait until the next. If you can realize what life would be like, if the thoughts of hatred or anger were made real in this life, then you will see that love is the only emotion we should extend to others. I feel sorry for people who are full of hatred against ethnic groups or other nations. They will have a tremendous amount of guilt when they go to the other side and realize how much time and energy they have wasted.

On one occasion a young man was brought through who hated white people. When I explained to him that it was his choice to be as he wished, so hating others was an excuse and it was also a choice. I sent out a thought for a black person to come and meet the young man and he went on to whatever destiny he desired.

There have been several runaway slaves who thought they were hiding, not realizing they had been killed. Sometimes the mind will be kind to a victim and hold back the painful memory of such a trauma. Sometimes the spirit has left the body before the physical life is terminated. In some cases the person brought for rescue will have difficulty recalling how he died. I don't press the issue, such memories are best forgotten.

I have been told by some of the guides that there are many people who have mistreated people from other ethnic groups and who were very remorseful when they realized what they had done. Some felt they needed to atone for their behavior to others, and insisted on reincarnating in the same ethnic group to experience the same situations as the ones they hated. Seems there are many crossover souls among us. Be careful how you treat your neighbor, you may be creating a problem for yourself.

One guide always shows himself as a Zulu warrior and is proud to do so. He told me that he had been a white doctor in French West Africa and had refused to treat the natives. When he got to spirit and saw what an opportunity he had missed to be of service to others, he insisted on reincarnating as a native in a similar situation. He became a witch doctor and was eventually killed in a tribal war.

We are responsible for our own thoughts and we can change our thoughts about a person or thing in an instant. Knowing this, you have the choice of selecting the kind of life you want. This is true on earth and it is also true in spirit. We always have the choice to accept or reject any situation.

To love oneself and to love others is the key to happiness. It may not be possible to love everybody but you can be kind to all people. Kindliness is beneficial to both the giver and receiver and teaches us that anger is destructive. I do believe that we get back the same emotions we project, and that is certainly true in the next states of awareness. When some fear is manifested and a frightful figure appears, all we have to do is send love or bless the apparition and it will transform before our eyes. This is one of the fun things that demonstrate the power of love to us.

Within all people is the divine spark that links us all to the creator of all things. We have to outgrow our negativity to go beyond the effects of the physical/astral planes and lose some of our beliefs about the nature of man. Again, we must remind ourselves that we create our own reality by the thoughts we think, and that we take our memories with us wherever we go.

Some people are so afraid of death that they will stay with the corpse after they die. They will hang around a cemetery after the funeral. Sensitive people passing a cemetery may see a specter or ghostlike figure hovering over a grave. In rescue work, when a person like that comes through, I explain that death is nothing to fear, and I send them on to their loved ones.

I find it easier to use such terms as "going to spirit," than to try to explain that we don't go anywhere when we die, we merely change our perception to another dimension. There is plenty of opportunity for a soul to learn about time/space/causality in spirit. My task is to get them over their illusions about life and death.

If we can have a belief in the divine origin of all beings, and know that we are all part of this great creative essence of energy and love, we will pass rapidly through the astral planes to the spirit world to our loved ones when we go to spirit.

Fortunately there is change and growth on every level of being and there is always help for those who ask for it.

CHAPTER SEVEN

THE POWER OF LOVE

IT IS DIFFICULT FOR US TO REALIZE there is only one universal force of creativity, which we call consciousness, and that it manifests in various ways as all that is. At the most spiritual level, at its highest expression, it is unconditional love, a state of non-relative beingness.

We enter into this dimension and set the universe up as a reality. The self interacts with this self/other relationship as co-creator of the feelings and sensations which give it validity. Our ultimate goal is to return to this original expression of unconditional love and be free of attachment to knowingness.

At the physical level we know love as an emotion, a pleasant feeling of approval of whatever we are experiencing. Man rarely thinks of love as a force or power of creativity capable of changing man at every level of his beingness.

Whether the love we feel is for a person or an object, or a piece of music, the reaction is very similar. It is good to be in the presence of, or have a thought of, the object of our attraction. At this emotional level love depends on a response. It can change very quickly to some other emotion if it is not acknowledged and accepted.

Scientifically we know that love has electrical and chemical properties. It is an electrical impulse passing across the synapses of the brain, resulting in a thought or feeling. This results in a chemical action on the brain and the nervous system, which affects the physical body. It is this flood of chemicals flowing through the physical system that gives these pleasurable feelings.

This information on the mechanics of love as an emotion has little to do with the spontaneity experienced from the wonderful feeling of being in love or expressing love to another person. The feeling of love when two people are attracted to each other is an automatic signal to all physical, emotional, and spiritual levels of awareness. It is a signal to the higher level of our being, to open us up to a direct expression of our inner self. Perhaps this is the reason we see only the more spiritual qualities and attractive aspects about the other person when we are sexually attracted to them.

We set aside certain days, such as Valentine's Day, to remind us of this romantic love, and we celebrate anniversaries such as Mother's day, which are dedicated to reminding us of our loved ones. Although this is commercialism at its worst, we learn from this experience the pleasure of giving, sharing, and hopefully, rekindling a commitment to another person.

It is truly amazing, the sudden onrush of feeling that sweeps over us and causes us to do things contrary to reason when we fall in love. Perhaps that's why we say a person is madly in love. If only we could prolong that blissful feeling.

Like any emotion, personal love can be turned on or off, depending on whether the object of our love is present, physically or mentally. The expectation of a chance meeting, or just remembering a previous experience with a loved one can cause those pleasant feelings to emerge again. The same is true of a religious experience where we submit to the divine impulse.

I have learned from my own experience in psychic studies, that there are levels of consciousness where only love exists. It is not the personal kind of love I have described above, but a kind of spiritual experience where there is a feeling of being totally accepted. In this heightened state there is a feeling of freedom or belonging without restriction. This is known as unconditional love, or spiritual love. Volumes of poetry are written about this kind of spiritual love, but it is our own experience of personal love that brings us closest to this spiritual level.

There are obviously levels of mental experience that are beyond the usual daily activities of eating and drinking, etc. The fact that these levels exist is obvious to anyone who has experienced love.

This means we can raise our consciousness by expressing love, to a level of awareness free from negativity and fear. Apparently this level is part of us now, but we have generally closed it off during this lifetime. I suspect there are people somewhere on the earth plane who can live at this level of unconditional love, but I doubt if they are living in the hustle and bustle of our Western culture.

It would seem that access to this level of awareness should be simple. All the books tell us that the power of love is within us. I know there can be a flood of the feeling of love arising from the heart center of our being, a point of pure consciousness where all sense of beingness is experienced in the present.

The great teachers tell us that all we have to do is to be physically, emotionally, psychically and spiritually still and this wonderful experience should appear. However, I think this means that what we are seeking is not of this world and we have to retreat within ourselves, stop the movie in the mind, get beyond the ego, and allow this love to manifest from within.

I'm sure we have all had the experience of daydreaming, where all association with the physical world disappears and we enter into a state of reverie. At that time there is a feeling of oneness with the whole life experience, and there is a feeling of serenity and peace that seems to pervade our whole being.

Unfortunately, these are fleeting moments but they do give an awareness that there are those states where there is only love. I think we have only to listen to the inner prompting of our higher self to realize this truth. Then we can allow this love to be a factor in our daily life.

If we could make spiritual love an automatic expression of our being, creating an aura of love around us, I think we would live lives of peace and joy. Then I believe we would be bringing on earth the same feeling of love that there is in heaven. These feelings are the ones that replenish us. They are the actions of the inner self, that delights in the expression of love through every level of our being. The descent of grace is one of those experiences.

One of the spontaneous expressions of love we can experience is the feelings we have for our children. We try to love them and guide them to give them the knowledge they will need in this complicated world. The great test of our love comes when it is time to sever the parental influence and send them out into the world to be taught by personal experience.

We can only show them the way. If they do not measure up to our hopes or expectations, we are naturally disappointed. We have to learn that all the good and the bad is for growth. We are not responsible for their personal choices, but if we have taught them the greatest lesson of all, to love oneself and others, then our task it completed.

This lesson of love is one thing we can pass on to others by our personal example. If we have been able to go through life with tolerance and understanding toward others, we will have enjoyed the trip and our children would have learned a priceless lesson.

We adopt belief systems, philosophies, nationalities, religions, and other divisive means of separating ourselves from our fellow man. We judge and discriminate against others and forget that the force that created us is shared by all, and it is love. We do have to feel it and project it, to know it.

It is easy to say we love everybody in an abstract way but we do have preferences. We naturally exercise these choices because we live in a world where we have to interact with the environment and have to make decisions regarding our lives.

The one quality we can all exhibit freely is acceptance of another's choice in life. Add to that an attitude of loving friendliness and tolerance and it will bring a similar response from others. I'm sure you have experienced how the attitude of another person affects you.

The guides and other teachers who come to instruct us, tell us that love is a combination of millions of facets of our total personality. Any attempt to pinpoint love, is trying to do the impossible. Love is a universal force for us to use, or not. So scientific explanations of the nature of love are purely academic. What really counts, where the exercise of the power of love is concerned, is intent. If an action is conditional on a response from another it is an investment. Love should be a gift and if we gain from it in some way, then it is not love.

In rescue work I have helped mothers who have killed their children and themselves to save the children from abuse or starvation. They felt life was hopeless and they were helpless; so, they took the only action they felt necessary. Their intent was good. When they found that there was no death, their guilt was terrible for them. One mother felt she should go to hell for what she had done and was looking for it. When I explained that there was no such place, she was confused. I quickly showed her the children with Sister Mary and an emotional reunion followed.

To feel the force of love is simple. Just close your eyes and visualize that the power of love is like a breeze coming from behind you. You will have the feeling of an infusion of love permeating your being. You may have the feeling that you can lean back against this force and have the pleasure of a sense of confidence and serenity. This little exercise can be done at any time, especially in times of stress. Or, stand in the wind and feel the breeze cleanse the aura of negativity. Feel the flow of unwanted conditions going away from you, and a feeling of peace and upliftment will come.

Sometimes in this world a person can get so confused that love becomes a tragedy. On a few occasions there have been cases where a young couple have committed suicide so they could spend eternity together, where their love would never die. A case of this nature came through quite recently. Their intent was to preserve their love and protect it from the cruelty of the world.

Quite often mothers will come through absolutely screaming and hysterical. This is especially true when a child is trapped in a fire, or when the child is suffering and the mother cannot reach the child. The parent is looking around at the scene of the incident, and the guides and loved ones cannot get to them. The mother is completely unaware that she too has died.

As I am still on the same earth plane vibration to which she is attaching herself, she will respond to me. Once I can get her to quiet down, I can explain to her that she is looking in the wrong direction. As soon as I can get her to look at the light, generally Sister Mary is there with the children or a grandparent will be there with them and another joyful reunion takes place.

Saving a soul in this kind of circumstance is one of the rewards of doing rescue work.

There is a love that is projected from the advanced souls on the higher planes which permeates the levels of awareness in which we can share. In meditation, a wonderful experience can be had if we ask our guides to take us to the level where there is only love.

The feeling of total acceptance by these spirit guides can have a humbling affect. Sometimes a person will feel that he should kneel before this love. The guides do not want such submission, they want only to serve us and help us in our quest. Regardless, I encourage students to acknowledge the presence of their guides, and to send thanks and love to them whenever they have been helpful.

It feels as if the power of love expressed at these higher levels can completely absorb us into itself, and it seems to call for a total surrender of the individual personality.

The surrender of the personality is necessary if we are to experience the higher states of beingness. We have to nullify, or get beyond, the ego. This is possible in meditation, or fervent prayer, or by withdrawing into the inner parts of our being.

It is as if we are poised on the edge of consciousness facing this third dimension. We can be aware of the presence of other levels of vibration around us, but until we turn and face within, to the source of the power, we will always be looking outward into this world. When asked how to find the kingdom of heaven, Jesus said, "You must give up this life, to find it." Obviously, this does not mean we should commit suicide. It means we should turn aside from the materialism of this life, and find the inner self which is the avenue to the higher levels of self-awareness.

In Christianity the practice of total surrender to God with a devotional, "Thy will, not mine" expression is an ideal way to feel the sensation of release from the earthly influences. Such self-abnegation will enable the seeker to find his own spiritual path. Any method of introspection should enable a person to enjoy unity with his higher self, but prayer or devotion to God will certainly bring a person to self-realization.

The use of mind-altering drugs will not bring the same type of experience that meditation does. The drug user is at the mercy of the drug, and cannot stop the affects until the drug wears off. Also, there is always the possibility of addiction.

In meditation a person can return to full consciousness and self-control at will. In meditation there are no bad trips or sudden flashbacks that can disturb the equilibrium and cause trouble. It is better to be sure of what is being done to our mind and body. They're needed in this state of worldly life.

CHAPTER EIGHT

INDIVIDUAL MEDITATION

IT IS POSSIBLE TO MEDITATE ANYWHERE but the most desirable situation is to create a place where there is a peaceful feeling. Many people have a special place for their meditation which is free of bright lights and noise, as a distraction will cause a loss of that peaceful atmosphere which is so necessary for a successful meditation.

A quiet state of mind that is free of disturbing thought is also desirable, for thoughts and emotions have to be subdued. I try to create an atmosphere of spiritual anticipation and as I enter the place where I am to meditate, I visualize I am passing through a screen of light which filters out negativity and the events of the day. I try to keep in mind that for the next period of time I will be attempting to raise my thoughts to a higher state of awareness.

It is also important to understand that we will be attempting to shift our attention to another dimension of consciousness where the inner senses are located. This means we have to withdraw our attention from the outer world and redirect it to the inner world as much as possible. We do this almost automatically when we go to sleep at night. We have to change our focus from this world to a sleep state, but this does not seem to require the type of concentration that meditation does.

This preparation of our mental state is preferred if we are to have a spiritual experience free of thought. The mind is like a non-stop movie and it hates control. If you have had a sleepless night, where the mind will not stop its activity, you will understand the need for the discipline and ritual.

The inner senses are located in the non-physical part of our being, the next level of awareness which is called the Astral Plane, or Dream State. This is the level of awareness we experience when we are out of our body during sleep. At this level we can gather much information, because people in spirit can communicate directly with us. Many people have had prophetic dreams that have had significant meaning later.

Meditation is a common practice in all religions. There may be many different names for the attempt we make to find the truth about ourselves, as well as many different techniques. Yet we are all seeking the same thing, which is to expand our sensitivity to experience another level of awareness.

Meditating on a religious symbol can be helpful. Having a mental picture of Jesus or some other saintly being will help to focus the mind's concentration. Meditating in a church or some place that inspires uplifting thoughts also helps to set the stage..

Generally speaking, there are four stages of progression, and the biggest problem is to get started and to have the necessary discipline for regular practice.

Stage 1. Attention. Bring the mind to the selected subject of meditation by limiting distractions. Our minds like to jump from subject to subject for no apparent reason. The flow of thoughts have to be brought under control before we can proceed.

I prefer a straight-backed chair which gives some support to my back. Many people prefer a yoga posture but I find that is difficult for my aging body. I believe that meditation should be completely free of tension or physical strain, for the object of the practice is to withdraw from the body and the ego-driven mind to a state of peace. A person cannot meditate if he has a physical ailment such as a toothache or a cold.

The method I like, is to sit comfortably with both feet on the floor, hands resting in my lap, and then become aware of my breathing. Being aware of the sense of touch at the edge of the nostrils, as the air goes in and out of the nose, will help to focus the attention. All the time I am aware of that sense of touch, there are no other thoughts in the mind. The moment a thought arises I know I have lost the concentration. I have to keep bringing my attention back to the stillness and the silence.

I found that mind chatter was difficult to stop because I had never attempted mind control before. It took a few weeks to find the silence, but eventually I was able to experience some success by finding the "NOW." It is that point between the past and the future, where I am seemingly balanced on the edge of a void. It was at this moment-point that I found peace.

Stage 2. Concentration. Here I had to learn how to focus on being focussed. I had not only to be attentive, but also to direct that attention upon the object of my meditation. I had to concentrate to the exclusion of all other thoughts. I had chosen the term, "Who am I" as a focal point and I kept repeating this mentally until it seemed like the "Who am" part disappeared. This left the "I" and I began to feel some physical and mental activity around me that was unusual.

I began to have a sensation of unreality, as if everything was becoming unstructured. I began to realize there was no longer stability in what I was seeing and I felt I was becoming a part of whatever was happening around me. I experienced a sense of peace and a complete loss of fear whenever I was able to find the "I AM" part of my being.

I began to realize there was an energy field around me and I could detect what seemed like clouds of colored energy floating around. I discovered later that this was called the aura which is a manifestation of the creative force that is the stuff that all things are made of.

By focussing on one point of light in the midst of this activity, I found I was entering the next stage. It seemed I could drift through a tunnel towards this light and I felt no fear at being drawn along. Somehow I knew I could stop the meditation and return to normal consciousness whenever I wished. The desire to know truth provided the impetus to keep going.

Stage 3. Meditation. This was a state of great revelation. I came to the realization that everything is composed of the same energy force. Nothing is excluded, and this force seems to manifest according to the laws appropriate to the level of the consciousness of the observer. It seemed that each level of experience had a different vibration rate; so, I surmised that this accounted for the time difference in the dream state.

On earth we call this force atomic energy and we know that everything we see is composed of this force and that the atomic structure determines the density and other characteristics of whatever I was aware of. I realized I was made of the same stuff as everything around me, and as I looked at an object it radiated an energy I could identify with.

This was the first step in meditation. The realization of the oneness of all things, including people. I began to realize how the individual mind made all the differences in people and things. Each of these steps was a revelation. I had difficulty understanding some of the concepts and changes in my thinking. I looked at, but could not understand some of the scientific books about the nature of man and the universe.

In meditation I felt there was no need for scientific journals and lectures because everything seemed understandable. If all things were variations of the same substance and were the result of the thoughts of the observer, all the theories were unnecessary.

Stage 4. Contemplation. At this stage I began to lose physical awareness but I was aware of being in a state where there was pure light. I felt this was the area where my journey to the earth had started. There was an intense feeling of love. I knew there was a creative essence here and that every thought I had, manifested. Somehow I knew I was in a very spiritual situation and I did not want to leave.

On one occasion I was in an altered state of awareness where there was pure light all around me. Suddenly I was aware of being in an energy field and there were hundreds of points of light floating all around. When I looked at one of these points of light, I entered into an incarnation experience. I found I could return to the core being whenever I wished and I could explore different incarnations without any feeling of attachment.

I had the feeling I was in a place from which we are attracted to the incarnation experience to come. I say this because I felt attracted to some of the points of contact and not to others. I believe that attraction is one of the elements of selection for our future experiences if we choose to have them. It seems we have free will even at this level. Then different thoughts began to come and I found I had to identify with the earthly vibration.

Whenever I had a thought, I would come back to this physical reality, elated, mystified and in awe of the experiences. I felt I had been in the presence of some supreme force or being that was formless but extremely powerful.

I know that level of consciousness is always there. It is a frame of reference from which a person can structure his life. I know I can never lose what I have discovered; so, I could turn my back on all I had learned and get on with this present life.

I decided I needed an education to help me understand the relevance of what I had experienced. So, at the age of thirty- seven, I went to college.

From the experiences of meditation my whole outlook on life has changed and I know now that I create my own reality by the thoughts I think. No longer can I blame exterior things for any misfortune in life. Everything I experience is the result of my opinion of how a thing is and what it means to me.

I began to experience some spontaneous mystical experiences. On one occasion I was listening to a radio program discussing the various ways that man uses music and rhythm. The speaker started talking about the development of musical instruments, and I began to experience a mind-altering state where I progressed through various types of music from jazz to the classics. Eventually, I was aware of hearing an angelic soprano singing a hymn of praise to God. Then, I heard beautiful music which I felt had not been written yet and I knew somehow I was in a state where the future had yet to manifest. I recall that some musicians claim they can touch a level of pure music when they are composing.

On another occasion I was withdrawn from normal awareness and I could see the atomic structure of everything around me.

The variations of density of the objects was the only difference in them. Everything was a mass of points of light. Again, I felt I was seeing a different level of manifestation of each object and I was seeing a level of an object before it manifested in earthly form.

Since those early days of revelation, I found great help from the teacher of a meditation group. He was able to guide me by answering my questions as they arose. I soon found I was able to help others; so, I formed a group of people who were asking me the same questions that I once had and we began a series of weekly meetings. I found that I learned along with the group and it was great fun to be in the company of like-minded people.

I have found the power of a group seems to multiply the energy level and meditation is easier. I find that seven to ten people is a good number to have and it is of no consequence what their religious or ethnic background is.

The most important ingredient of the group is the attitude of the sitters. We are what we think we are and we create an atmosphere around us. If that atmosphere is negative, then the whole group can be affected. The object is to create a circle of love in which the personal attributes of the sitters loses its importance. A group should be open to anyone who meets the criteria of being a seeker after the truth and is willing to enter the silence to find it.

If we look around any group we may be thinking of joining, we will recognize that we have all come together for the same purpose. We are all seeking self-fulfillment, so we put aside personal prejudices to realize we are there to share. It is important that each person realize that he can disrupt the entire group if he is on an ego trip.

Take what the group has to offer but be sure to contribute your love and energy. Life or spiritual growth is not a competition. We are all on the same path and are walking it in our own particular way.

When you feel you have outgrown the group, you will move on. Take what you have learned and share it with others. It matters not what you teach, as you can only relate the truth as you know it.

All is in a process of change. What we believe today may change tomorrow. Do not feel guilty if you think you have mislead someone else. They will determine their belief system based on their total experience of life, not on what you may tell them. However, you can help another person on the path by some exchange of personal experiences. It's a wonderful feeling to know you have helped another person raise their understanding to a new level.

It would be nice if we could teach the perfect truth, but perfection means that we have reached the end of the road and there is nowhere else to go. That, of course, is wrong. The growth process is exactly that, a process of change.

Sometimes we may sit for a long time and nothing seems to be happening. Progression is like being on a flight of steps, each level is like a plateau and we only move on to the next one when the knowledge of the present one is fully absorbed.

Impatience is both a positive and a negative condition. Positive in that it indicates you are eager to go on, and negative in that we have lost the sense of peace of mind essential to moving on. Thus, we must accept where we are before we can outgrow our need to be where we are.

One of the most common barriers to growth is spiritual pride. The idea that one person is better that another, because of a little more knowledge, leads to many problems. I have found that some of the greatest teachers and guides in spirit are humble and wish only to be recognized as equals. I remember my own teacher, when I said to him, "Brother Peter, I could listen to you for hours." He replied,

"My son, I do not want your ears, I want your hands to go and do the work of healing." He is a great being who has taken the trouble to help those of us on the earth who are willing to listen.

There are many wonderful teachers in the spirit world who love to come and teach us about life beyond the grave. They tell us that we have access to all the truths about reality if we would only look within ourselves. Within us is the key to the inner senses that will put us in touch with our guide who is waiting for us to make contact.

Like most people I studied everything I thought would be of help in my quest, but the truth is within each of us. If we could follow the directions of the heart we would be completely in tune with the infinite. The heart of our being is in the heart center, not the physical organ, but the center of our being. This center is in another state of awareness which can be reached through the practice of meditation. The heart center is the link with that divine part of our being from which we draw our substance.

After several years of meditation practice, the knowledge that love is the primary force of creation becomes a natural way of looking at things. It seems as if our total concept of who we are changes, and the personal experience of this world takes on a different meaning.

We will see opportunities of service to mankind wherever we look and we will do things because they need to be done, not for personal gain. The only true happiness in life comes from such service, for all things are transitory. The knowledge that we are part of the creative process should bring a sense of freedom, not of bondage. If we can see the oneness of all things, then the calmness of the acceptance of life comes like the descent of grace.

Meditation will show the way to the inner senses and open doors that let us into higher states of being. But we must look within to find it.

CHAPTER NINE

HOW TO MEDITATE
Suggestions for Beginners

THE PURPOSE OF MEDITATION is to make a consciousness shift and withdraw your attention from this three dimensional world and allow yourself the opportunity to experience other levels of awareness. To achieve this you need the right conditions. The physical setting as well as the right mental attitude is of help in enabling you to concentrate on the task of meditation.

It is important that you find a quiet place, free of any distractions, such as loud noise or bright lights, to allow a shift of awareness from this world to another level of awareness. The atmosphere should give you a feeling of spiritual uplift and peace. You will need a comfortable seat, one that gives support to your back. Sit with both feet on the ground and let your hands rest on your lap. Or adopt the yoga lotus position if you are familiar with it. The aim is to be completely comfortable with your position, so you can disregard the physical body and the room, and transfer your complete attention to an inner reality.

There are many audio tapes available which will help you to meditate, or you can make your own using the following meditation which I use for all new classes. Once you become aware of the process you will develop your own procedure.

Most people find that listening to another's voice helps with relaxation. You may wish to make your own tape, or have someone else make one for you. Experiment with different voices to find one you are comfortable with.

Record the following, allowing a pause after each statement to allow yourself time to experience the effects of the changes that should take place in your feelings and attitude.

* * * * *

With your eyes closed, become aware of the life force flowing through your veins.

Feel the power of this life force which permeates every cell of your body. This is the great creative spiritual force within you. Without this force you would not be alive in this dimension.

Direct your attention to your breathing. Breathe normally, easily, no strain, feel relaxation as you breathe out.

Generally, you do not pay attention to the autonomic faculties such as our breath and heart beat; however you are now taking control of these processes and they are becoming noticeable.

Become aware of the flow of air as it goes in and out of your nose. Notice the sense of touch at the edge of your nostrils. (This will help you focus your attention.)

Notice how the mind is clear while you are aware of the air flow.

(If a thought arises in your mind, you will have lost your concentration. Don't try to suppress any thoughts, when you find your mind wandering, bring your attention back to the edge of your nostrils. Keep doing this until you can focus your attention for about two or three minutes.)

The object of this exercise is to clear the mind of all association with this physical world, to stop the stream of thoughts running through your mind.

(Once you have learned how to concentrate your attention you will be able to shift your focus to any part of the body. There is no law that says your point of awareness must reside in the head. It can be wherever your attention is directed.)

Now, shift your focus from your nose to the center of your head. Visualize that this point of awareness is like a beacon radiating light outward in every direction.

You are the power that creates the light, and I want you to try to withdraw your attention to be in the center of the beacon.

Feel the light surrounding you.

(This will bring you in touch with the next level of consciousness which is the dream state or astral plane. You may have some feelings of disorientation and this is quite natural and normal. You may become aware of some psychic activity around you and you may be tempted to interact with it, try not to.)

You are beginning to shift your awareness to this next dimension and the vibration rate is a little different, a little faster.

All the senses usually become enhanced and there is a strong feeling of the life energy flowing through your veins.

As you breathe in, think the words I AM, and as you breathe out, think the word RELAXED.

With each outward breath, allow yourself to go deeper.

Let go of tension. It is a feeling as if you are going down in an elevator into a deeper part of yourself.

Relax as much as you can. (Ignore any psychic activity.)

While in this relaxed state let me ask you, "What are you aware of?" You may be aware of your feet touching the floor, or of your seat touching the chair, or of your fingers if they are touching something.

You may have noticed that your attention immediately went to the part of the body I mentioned. This helps you to see that you are, in some respects, where your attention is directed.

Direct your attention to the center of your head and focus on the act of just being conscious, just being aware.

Now I ask you, "Who is it that is being aware?"

You will notice that this point of consciousness is in the center of a vast open field, stretching in all directions to infinity, for you are the center of your universe. You can extend your awareness to infinity for the mind is limitless.

"Again I ask you, who is aware of this experience?"

That point or part of you that notices everything is not like anything else. "How do you know it is there?"

I want you to be aware that you are seeking one permanent, unchanging observer of all that is going on around you.

"Who is that observer?"

(These questions should bring a mental response of "I AM".)

Just experience a sense of beingness in the here and now.

Mentally check to see that no tension has crept back into the body.

To reach the NOW it will help if you imagine you are riding on the crest of a wave of time, which is moving across an ocean of life experience.

The past is behind you and there is nothing you can do about that. The future hasn't happened yet; so, don't be concerned with that.

The only thing you can be really sure of is NOW the existential moment.

In the NOW is the I AM, in pure beingness.

Any thought arising in the mind gets in the way of the sense of pure experience. Don't try to suppress any thought, just let it float away.

Life, or the future, is ever coming toward you, becoming the now, then going into the past.

Life only becomes a reality when you identify with what is going on around you.

Notice how you can be involved or detached, as you choose.

Notice how you create your own interpretation of reality by the thoughts you think.

You determine the thoughts in your mind by your reaction to stimulation from inside or outside of the body.

Prove this to yourself by sending love to someone that you care for.

Notice the effects, the warm feeling, from sending love to another.

Now send anger to them; notice the difference, the tension.

Send love to them again. Let's not leave them in anger.

From this exercise you will see how you can choose the emotions you will feel if you have control of your thoughts.

You can determine the person you will be by the quality of the thoughts that you think.

Don't think any more. Just relax in a state of beingness with your mind directed to the infinite, through the center of your forehead or the crown of your head.

Throughout your life you have been seeking something, seeking experience at all levels, trying to find out who you are, do you fit in, are you acceptable.

I suggest to you that the thing that you are seeking is the thing that is doing the seeking.

THE THING YOU ARE SEEKING IS THE THING DOING THE SEEKING.

You have been seeking to make the inner self real.

Allow yourself to be immersed in the light of this inner self and let the higher self direct your meditation.

At this spiritual level just be an observer of what is happening around you; try not to participate.

Rest here for a few moments.

Your inner self will bring you back to a dreamlike state when the meditation is completed.

Now when you are ready, bring yourself back to full awareness of the room where you are meditating and sit quietly while you recall any significant feelings or ideas from your meditation.

* * * * *

Do not expect immediate results. You have to overcome the desire to be involved with everything going on in the meditation. It is necessary to sit quietly for a few moments after a meditation and try to remember any significant results of your experience; otherwise, you will not recall what has happened. By thinking of those events you will be recording them in your memory bank.

While in the meditation, you may have become aware that the thing that you were seeking, or the I AM, precedes every thought, every feeling, every aspect of this life. It is the central thought of your being.

The thought that we create our own reality by the thoughts we think should not be an awesome realization. It should bring a sense of freedom.

In future meditations you will experience a surrender of the self and you will begin to have some unusual sensations.

You will be aware of some physical tingling sensations in and around the head and perhaps in other parts of the body. This is nothing to be worried about. It means you are becoming aware of the inner senses as you shift consciousness from one level to another.

The rate of vibration on the earth is slower than that of the dream state, or astral plane. It is as if we have to speed up our sense of awareness to that of the faster vibration. This is the consciousness shift we have been seeking. It is this difference in vibration that creates the separation between the levels of awareness. Becoming aware of our inner energy centers opens us up directly to the higher levels of consciousness and will eventually unite us with our higher self.

In time, and with regular daily practice, you will become aware of a light that surrounds you. It may appear as a point of light at first but you will soon see it expand and you will be aware of being in the center of a ball of energy. This is the magnetic field around you, the aura.

The aura is a level of energy from the next state of awareness. It is only relevant to the physical and astral planes and can be discounted as it contains emotions and desires associated with the earth plane; therefore, our quest is to raise our consciousness to a higher level, free of such attachment.

Each person is immortal and indestructible. The only thing that changes when we withdraw from this plane, is our perception. We automatically adjust to the level of consciousness we have tuned into. The whole atmosphere changes and we realize that we are in another dimension. Regardless of the level of consciousness, we find we have the appropriate form with which to express ourselves.

On the earth plane we can change our self-image by a change in our attitudes. The same is true in the astral and spirit worlds except that in these other states our thoughts, feelings and attitudes manifest instantly. There are no secret thoughts in spirit.

Through meditation we learn that the physical and astral planes are ego-driven. In the higher levels of consciousness we are responsive to and part of the creative process. In short, reality is a projection of ourselves.

In the third dimension we use the physical body composed of atoms. In the dream state or astral plane we use a duplicate of the physical body, a thought form created by our recollection of who we think we are on the earth plane. In the spirit world we usually maintain an image of ourselves to share experiences with loved ones.

We receive training in the use of the powers that we had before we assumed this present identity and we learn more of the nature of beingness.

After we have outgrown the spirit world and its attachments, we are ready to enter higher planes where the use of form is optional. At these higher levels of awareness we are a point of light and energy with creative power and we have the ability to choose what we project as our image for recognition purposes.

One day, as I came into Los Angeles by plane, I could not see the ground because of the smog. I thought how similar it is to being on the higher planes and looking out to the earth plane. On the earth plane we are not aware of being in an extension of other worlds. Obviously our sense of reality in this dimension is based on what we can see around us.

It may not be possible for you to devote a lot of time to meditation, but I have it on good medical authority that if you get up half an hour earlier to meditate, you will not drop dead. If it really is not possible for you to meditate daily try the next exercise.

One simple procedure I recommend to friends is to tune in to spirit when you arise in the morning. Visualize that there is a light above your head, shining down upon you. This light is full of love, energy and spiritual power. Bring the light down through the body and imagine that it is permeating every cell of your body, just as if it were the sun shining down on you. Feel the life force coursing through your body which is being reinforced by this great gift of love from spirit.

I use the image of the sun because it shines on everyone equally, without discrimination, and asks for nothing in return. This is also true of spiritual power, and of unconditional love.

This simple exercise awakens you to your divinity, to your spiritual heritage and makes you realize you are part of a great experience in this level of consciousness. Within a week of this practice you will feel this is a necessary part of your daily preparation and it will set you up for the day. I often have the thought, "Let's see what life has for me today."

Naturally a period of time in meditation is best, but to have something like this exercise in your memory bank for times of stress is useful. Anytime you are under stress at work, just close your eyes for a few seconds while you visualize this divine energy sweeping down over you. Feel the peace that comes from within and you will feel refreshed.

CHAPTER TEN

A PERSONAL SEARCH
FOR TRUTH

IN MY SEARCH FOR TRUTH I attended many meetings and listened to many speakers on the subject of Spiritualism. I also read a number of books on Eastern and occult philosophies. I came to realize that the only way to satisfy my curiosity was to have personal experience of the higher planes of consciousness. This meant meditation and introspection.

I joined a development group taught by Harold Sharp, a spiritualist medium, and learned that the best way to extend the sensitivity of my consciousness was to begin a regular meditation practice at home. I began to meditate twice daily. Immediately after I got out of bed in the morning I would meditate for an hour, and again before going to bed I would repeat the practice.

At first little happened and I thought I could not do it. Then one night after meditating for an hour, I was sitting up in bed and the door opened and a monk walked around the bed, sat on a seat and smiled at me. I laid down in the bed and left the body immediately and went with him into another state of awareness.

I had no fear at all and, unfortunately, I have no idea of anything that happened during the time I was unconscious. This is often the case with out-of-body experiences.

Sometimes I can recall things in retrospect after an excursion into other planes, but during the experience and after the event, there is often no recollection. I think it depends on the level, or degree, of separation attained. The activity close to the earth vibrations seems easier to recall, as in a dream. The higher quality experiences appear to be too far removed from our level of awareness for easy recall.

I discovered later that I had been in an altered state of consciousness. The door had not opened physically, what I had seen was called an astral plane experience where a duplicate door was opened and I was seeing a spirit figure who had come to see me. I had not realized it, but I was in the altered state from my meditation and was in a suitable frame of mind for an out-of-body experience. I suspect it was one of my guides who had come to teach me that I did not need a physical body to be alive, except in this third dimension.

Like most people, I had many dreams, some very vivid. I know this experience was not a dream. I felt I was in full control of my senses and was not asleep until my head hit the pillow.

On another occasion I had finished meditating; then, and out of the corner of my eye I saw two figures reflected in a mirror across the room. If I looked directly at them, they disappeared. I soon realized I was using peripheral vision. After some practice I found I could see spirit people by using this type of peripheral vision. They seemed to overshadow the features of the person I was looking at.

Sometimes it seemed as if I could see right through a person and I could see the spirit figure instead of the physical person. I had the feeling of a different sense of awareness when this happened. It is as if I am disoriented slightly from the usual earthly conscious state. I think we can sometimes be aware in more than one level of consciousness. I call this being bi-located, and it can happen spontaneously to anyone. Hallucinations and visions during periods of reverie are good examples of mind expansion.

I discovered later that the overshadowing I could see was an image of a being from spirit projected into the aura of the person I was looking at. Everything in this experience seemed to be happening normally but I soon learned that I had switched to another level of perception in the next dimension.

Every object has an energy field surrounding it which is part of the person or thing. This auric atmosphere can be used by spirit people to manifest what are known as thought-forms. Apparently this energy field surrounding a person can be imprinted by the thoughts of people in spirit. Mediums and sensitive people can see these forms, and this is one method of thought transference that is used in spirit communication.

Then began a series of out-of-body experiences. At first they happened spontaneously and I found myself free of the body in my own bedroom. As I disengaged from the body there was a rush of energy inside me and my body seemed charged with electricity. I found I had only to think of the sensation and it would happen again and I could take off. I learned the sensation was an energy change from the earth vibration to the vibration of the astral plane. I later discovered there are many groups who regularly practice what is called astral projection and there are many books on this extraordinary subject.

On one occasion I was about to leave the bedroom through the wall when I had the thought, "What if there is nothing there?" I went through the wall into complete blackness. Then, I had a thought, "There should be a tree outside my window," and it appeared. I found I could create anything I wanted, go anywhere I wanted, within reason. I tried to visit the White House and was barred in some way. I think notable people have to be protected from the intrusion of curiosity seekers.

It soon became obvious that the mind has an image-creating ability we can all use, and it comes into play more readily in the astral plane. I later realized that all these experiences were preparation for the future, and I was going through what happens to many people when they die.

The realization that I could exist without a physical body helped me to understand that there are many planes of awareness which we are not aware of until an experience like mine takes place. I also discovered that we go to the level of existence to which we are compatible.

I found in the astral plane, there are levels of darkness and despair, a level of anger and violence and a level of fear. There are also levels of joy and love, beauty and music. Flowers project their colors from within and do not need the reflected sunlight as earthly flowers do.

I found that the astral plane responds to the atmosphere of the observer. Where music is concerned, if I am thinking of spiritual aspiration, I hear spiritual music. Otherwise I hear orchestral music that seems to suit my taste. Generally it is music that has not been written on earth, as far as I know.

I knew somehow that when I left the body I was protected and I also knew that I had things to do in the future. At that time I had no idea of rescue work, and it was ten years later that I became involved in this fascinating subject.

I studied the works of some of the mystics and found there are three methods by which the a mystical experience can be achieved. I studied the Christian approach of self-abnegation, the Zen Buddhist method of seeking the void, and the Yoga approach of introspection and self-analysis. I found that the end result of each method was the same. All religions are like the spokes of a wheel, all paths leading to the same truth which is in the heart or the hub of the wheel.

Some mystical experiences began to occur and each time I discussed them with my teacher. Having a competent teacher with experience in meditation was a great asset and I recommend it for anyone beginning an inner journey.

Nothing can compare to a personal experience. I wish I could convey to everyone the wonders of these levels of inner consciousness. We can know the existence of these spiritual levels of awareness, unfortunately we are usually looking in the wrong direction and our language does not contain the appropriate words. I can only tell people that they will make the same discoveries when they leave this plane.

From the studies I have done I realize there are many avenues to inner awareness. The most common are through prayer, meditation or out-of-body experiences similar to the ones described in this book. Anyone with dedication and discipline can achieve these goals. Do not think these things only happen to chosen people. I have found that there are many people who have studied mysticism and found truth but they will not talk about it to everyone.

In prayer we look outward to some superior force or being, and we tend to put the responsibility for our growth on some divine influence. In Christianity we are directed to seek the kingdom of heaven through devotion or faith. I found that fervent aspiration was a great help in explaining how the truth of the devotion and faith approach occurred.

I discovered a state of awareness where I could know the experience of the descent of grace. I was meditating one day and decided to try to send love to God. I used the "Thy will, not mine" approach of total surrender and it worked beautifully. I found myself in a pure golden light, and knew I was in a state of unconditional love and bliss.

In this heightened state of awareness I knew the oneness of all things. I realized that everything was in its right place and that separateness was the cause of most of man's problems. Things such as individuality, gender, race, religion or nationality all contribute to our sense of separation. I have found that the feeling of the presence of spirit in our daily life can make this earth life a wonderful experience.

The experience of the "Born again Christians" who find a rebirth and a new meaning in life because of the realization of the presence of infinite love within themselves, is a good example of spontaneous self-realization. Many mystics have reported the awakening of this force of love from within that comes from the result of prayer and meditation.

In all meditation the seeker attempts to reach a state of awareness where he can find the answers to the eternal questions of life. This requires a consciousness shift to another dimension and here the quest becomes difficult. The practice takes hours and calls for a discipline which the impatient seeker finds frustrating.

Eventually, I settled on a belief system that seemed to suit my temperament. Being guided to Spiritualism by a series of coincidences has helped to broaden my concept of reality. What I find desirable about Spiritualism is that it is eclectic and accepts people from all faiths. There are no rigid conditions of membership, no baptism or other rituals to be followed.

One thing I had to overcome was a reticence to pray to some unseen God. I thought that prayer was unnecessary because if God knew everything, why pray? Fortunately I had a good teacher and some early mystical experiences to show me the power of prayer. I quickly realized I was praying to my own higher self. I was really asking for understanding and guidance from my own inner self.

I found that prayer and meditation are avenues to the infinite, regardless of the religious beliefs of a person. Every religion has had its mystics who gave divine teachings to those who would listen and they mostly speak of meditation.

I found the physical, emotional, and spiritual benefits from the realization of the presence of the divine power within is immeasurable, so is the feeling of well-being that comes from the knowledge that there is something or someone who cares.

Some people have had a near-death experience or a mystical vision where they have been mentally lifted to a higher state of awareness. They have met discarnate individuals they have known on earth. This same experience can be achieved by psychic development or fervent aspiration to the divine. The ego can be bypassed and entry to the inner self discovered.

Ever since the days of the Greek philosophers, we have been encouraged to follow the edict over the gates at Delphi which was "Man know thyself." I must confess that when I went to Delphi, I went to the great amphitheater where the Oracle and great teachers and thinkers held their meetings and I could not find any inscription or gates. Of course the idea of knowing oneself is still valid.

Spiritual literature is full of techniques on how to extend ones sensitivity to communicate with the higher self or with other spirit beings. The books are merely rephrasing the teachings of the ancient masters who have said that the kingdom of heaven is within and that we should be still, and know the "I AM" is the way to the truth and the light.

Meditation will bring the seeker in touch with the infinite essence of creation, that all powerful force we call God. In the silence will come the realization that the thing we are seeking is the thing that is doing the seeking. For we are seeking that inner reality free of attachment to the ego-driven physical realm. Meditation on the divine spark within will bring what we are seeking which is self-realization.

It is extremely beneficial to our mental health to take some time each day to withdraw from the outer world. We can choose to go within, and to find what is really important about the self, as well as what we are doing in this life. If we can meditate and be receptive to the guidance of our higher self, we can find the answers to all those spiritual questions about life.

Sometimes, during the search for truth, I found I was apparently at a standstill and nothing was happening. After awhile things began to progress again, and I realized that progress was like ascending a flight of stairs, I could not move on until I had fully absorbed the plateau where I was. We outgrow our need to be where we are.

It appears difficult for those in spirit to communicate with us when we are engaged in our daily activities because we are outer-directed. However, in the silence of a meditation we can open ourselves to the prompting of our guides and teachers and feel the power of the love they bring to us.

I always advise students who come to me of my three golden rules. Keep your feet on the ground, let common sense be your guide, and your money the last thing you part with. Try not to let anyone deter you from your path and don't listen to the superstitions of others. Soon the truth of your identity will emerge from within and everything will fall into place.

A god-conscious period each day reminds us of our heritage and our divinity. I have found a morning meditation, before the affairs of the day cloud our vision, can be very helpful in creating a balance in life. In moments of stress, tune in to your inner self and find the peace and the love that is always there for you.

CHAPTER ELEVEN

EXPLORING THE ASTRAL PLANE

IN THIS HUMAN STATE OF AWARENESS there are unique qualities of experience available which make life here on earth
seem very attractive to some beings in spirit. Many souls
are attracted out of curiosity because they can experiment
and materialize situations they have thought about in other
levels of consciousness. The limitations imposed on a
person in this dimension create an intense learning atmosphere.

Conditions such as gender, environment, culture, and
personal physical limitations create needs and drives that
force the emergence of a new personality. The result is
growth through adjustment, enlightenment and understanding.

To create the best atmosphere for this new experience,
it is usually necessary to eliminate or sublimate most of the
memory of any past life experience. Previous experience
could influence the present incarnation and inhibit the
desired learning situation and prevent the use of free-will.

When possible a suitable entry point is selected to
ensure the realization of the hidden agenda of the person
incarnating. It is given to few people to know the real

purpose of their life. Such factors as time and place of incarnation are very important. Sometimes an entity will take on more than he can handle and will incarnate into a life that is frustrating and unsatisfying.

After the birth process is completed, a person may be very surprised by the severity of the restrictions in this physical world. Previously, they have not had to feed a body, or protect it from the environment. Sleep was never a necessity in the other planes and limitations of movement on this earth plane requires much adjustment for the incarnating spirit. There are many conflicting and confusing messages coming to the newborn which some find overwhelming. Some even find it better to withdraw and return to spirit.

Once the person has adopted the intense concentration necessary to maintain his presence here; then, much of the frustration is overcome and the person settles into this restrictive third dimension and adjusts to the give and take of this world.

The higher self constantly urges the person to seek self-fulfillment from the experiences he planned for himself; then, at the same time quietly reminds him of his spiritual heritage. It is the subtle influences from the higher self that create the seeming conflict between the person's desire for self-expression and the wish to return to spirit. Fortunately, there is access to other levels of consciousness that allow a person to experience other planes and the earth plane at the same time.

The most obvious example of extended sensitivity of awareness is the dream state. We take our memory into the dream world and recreate most of the physical plane we remember. The atmosphere often appears misty and forms may be indistinct. However, the dream world can also seem as durable as this one appears to be. There are rules to be observed in any state of awareness, and the dreamer quickly realizes that this first outer ring of activity beyond the physical level responds to his thoughts.

This next level of awareness is also known as the astral plane. It is an ideoplastic world where the dreamer's emotions and desires are materialized and he learns to outgrow some of the fears and other feelings he has accumulated in this earth life.

One observable activity of the astral plane is the radiation around a person which is called the aura. It contains colors and lights and is regarded as one of the levels of awareness between the physical and spirit worlds. It is part of the creative process and is a link between the various states of awareness we can experience while we are still in a physical body.

The duplicate body we exhibit in our dreams and in other out of body experiences, is a part of the total expression of the divine emanation of God in man. There has to be a link between the various planes, and the astral body with its aura is one of them. All the great teachers have told us that, "The Kingdom of Heaven is within us." I believe these various levels are the pathway to this realization.

In this astral plane is a system of energy centers which are links to all the different levels of being. Each center has a color associated with it and the brightness or quality of the color reflects the emotional state of the person at that time.

These centers approximately follow the line of the spinal column and extend just beyond the outer shell of the physical body. Each center is like a morning glory, or a saucer shaped disc of vibrating energy and color. Each energy center has a distinct vibration rate. This rate increases as we go through the different levels from the base of the spine to the crown of the head.

Starting with the one at the base of the spine is the one associated with the physical body. It has the color red, ranging from a dark red flecked with black streaks, to a delicate bright pink. The emotions of a person affect these centers and a clairvoyant person can determine the emotions of a person at any particular time. This is the only center which faces the rear of the body.

The second energy center is at the level of the umbilical cord. It has an orange color and is associated with the nervous system at the physical level, and the emotions at the mental level. A sudden shock or trauma can sometimes be felt like a blow to the stomach where this center is located.

Next, is the center at the level of the solar plexus and has a yellow color. This one is linked to the intellect and the activity of the mind on the brain. The thought process may be enhanced and recall may be greatly improved. A concentration on this center will usually bring a mild sensation of an electrical energy around the head.

At the center of the chest, at the breastbone level, is the green colored center. It is the first of the non-physical centers and it gives us an awareness of our aura and the astral plane atmosphere. It is at this level that we can sense the presence of loved ones from spirit trying to contact us.

At the throat level is the light blue colored center and it is linked to psychic hearing. Meditation on this center will bring an awareness of voices from spirit.

Sometimes a person will experience an echo of their own thoughts, as if their thoughts were repeated back to them. Sometimes a person may hear their name called when they are in a relaxed frame of mind. With a little practice it is easy to differentiate between the sources of communication.

Next, is the third eye which is like a dark blue morning glory, it is situated in the center of the forehead and is the center from which we send out thoughts and prayers. It is involved in mental telepathy and all other psychic activity. Through this center we can see into other states of awareness and have profound mystical experiences. Communication with loved ones in spirit is conducted through this center.

Projecting upward from the center of the head to the crown, is the seventh center and it is our link with the infinite. It is a large violet colored disk with a golden center. Above the head of each person is a golden light. From this light there is a ray of energy projecting through the system from which the various energy centers are powered. This center is the ultimate link with the divine while we are still conscious in the physical body.

A good meditation to get in touch with the higher levels of consciousness, is to start a concentration at the base of the spine and slowly work up through the system of energy centers.

If you would like to try this as a meditation, direct your attention to the area of the center described above and pause at each one for a few slow breaths while you imagine you are breathing in and out of each of the centers. Visualize you are withdrawing from this earth plane level of awareness to a more spiritual level.

In this astral plane the dreamer, or explorer, may be aware of the fact that he is dreaming and that he has the ability to change the environment around him. In rescue work this is a very common experience, especially for those who were deprived of material things in their past lives. They can create surprising fantasies and can play out many desires. In this astral plane, a sleeping person can release pent up emotions. Expression of some repressed fears and desires which arise in our daily life may prevent some stress.

Most dream experiences are spontaneous but the ability to leave the body consciously may be achieved with training. This is known as an out-of-body-experience (OOBE). When a person does project from the physical body, he realizes conclusively, that he can have a conscious experience of being alive, without the use of a physical body. There is nothing more evidential than this realization, that there are other planes of awareness similar to the earth plane.

The traveller will usually find himself in the astral plane. At first, the atmosphere appears rather dim, like a twilight. Then things become lighter and brighter as he gains confidence and learns how to function in the new experience.

In some Eastern religions, the astral plane is known as the emotion/desire plane, here is where a person outgrows many of his desires and attachments to the earth plane.

Upon release from the body, a person will see the dreamers. They are still locked into the earth plane as they are dealing with the effects caused by situations on earth. A person can go from an ecstatic experience to a nightmare in a few seconds.

This need to continually deal with things pertaining to the earth plane makes the dreamer mostly unaware of where he is. He may suddenly disappear as he is recalled to the sleeping body. Sometimes during an out-of-body experience there may be a disturbance in the bedroom, and the astral body is immediately pulled back. I have been recalled by a leg cramp or some outside noise, for example.

When a person tries to bring back memories of dream world experience there is usually distortion as the two planes do not have the same vibration.

The next group to be seen are those who have died and who are not yet aware of the fact. These entities are still focussed on their previous lives and have yet to make contact with those who have come to greet them. Many of these souls are looking for help and may be in a state of denial about their demise, and are unaware of the fact that they are refusing to go on to the loved ones waiting for them.

Close to this group are those who have discovered they can create things and they like to play with this new found power. They can become extremely possessive of their creations and will try to protect themselves with snakes, guns, dogs, fences and anything imaginable to keep out intruders. They are allowed to live this fantasy for awhile and then they are brought to a rescue worker for help. They only need a change in their perception of where they are, and what their needs are, then they can go on to join their friends.

The next group to be encountered are the greeters. They receive souls who come to the spirit world and who are seemingly lost. The greeters will help any being get adjusted and will help them make appropriate contacts for advancement or reunion with their loved ones.

Children who arrive and have no one in spirit to meet them, are cared for by beautiful beings; then, they are taken to levels where they can be encouraged to grow up and await the arrival of family members.

Eventually all souls are able to reach the realms of spirit, beyond the astral plane, where they are free of attachment. It is necessary for everyone to have outgrown many earth-related ideas, and it is also here that great learning and understanding takes place.

This is the area where many souls are seeking guidance beyond the earth plane influence. As soon as a person sends out the thought that they need help, they are contacted by guides who help them. A thought is projected as a flash of energy, or light, which is picked up by helpers who are always available to come and help.

It is in the spirit world, beyond the astral plane, that souls meet those who have gone through this process before. Here they will become aware of the oneness of all things and they will be able to see the reasons behind many of the problems they had in their previous lives. They will see that there is a reason for everything that has happened. No one will judge another person. Differences are resolved and souls are able to take an objective view of things.

In rescue work there are many situations where a person will have great anger toward someone they think has wronged them. As soon as they are tuned into the new vibration of the spirit world their anger disappears. It seems that human emotions belong to the earth plane and the astral plane, and we are not able to go into the spirit world until we have outgrown the need of these encumbrances.

In this spirit world are many levels of potential experience and time will be spent here, reviewing the lessons of the previous incarnations. There is much to be explored and enjoyed and plenty of opportunity to help others who are coming over.

There is very little understanding in traditional religions about the astral planes. Many souls are conditioned by religion to believe they must be judged, or they must wait for some saint or being to take them to some heavenly paradise. Such is not the case. Life is a continuation in spirit because we take our memory and character with us when we die.

One significant thing in the astral plane is the fact that people do not seem to age. I have helped people who would be hundreds of years old in earth time but they still exhibit the age they remember being when on earth. When I tell them they have been dead for hundreds of years, they may have a little difficulty accepting it, but they don't suddenly go through any changes. Age, it seems, is the expectation of, and an acceptance of change, in the growth process of the earth plane.

One of the great lessons to be learned in the astral plane experience is the power of love. As our emotions are manifested in tangible form, our fears will create objects such as monsters or animals that attack us. If this happens, we have only to bless them or to send love to the object; then, it will go through many transformations and eventually manifest as a pure expression of love. "As a man is in his heart, so is he," said Jesus.

This ability to create our own reality applies at every level of consciousness. Our emotions and desires take a little longer to manifest in this third dimension because we have to conform to its natural laws. Yet, the principle is the same, for as we project attitudes, others will respond accordingly.

There are many levels of experience in the astral plane and there are some which I call planes of desolation. Some people who die in a state of despair seem to have no desire to continue living. They create an atmosphere around them with a negative attitude that keeps helpers away; so they will wallow in this feeling of self-pity for long periods of time. This especially applies to suicides who have tried to end it all.

These people are kept together in an atmosphere of self-created darkness where they can hide for as long as they wish. Of course they are unaware of where they are and the possibilities which are available for them to receive all the help they need. Eventually, they are helped by guides or rescue workers who are willing to go into the darker planes to get them out.

This is the emotion/desire plane and you can imagine the type of atmosphere created by some people who never resolved lust and other similar feelings on the earth plane. There are some wonderful beings working to free those who are trapped by their own carnal desires.

In rescue work, the people brought to me are people that I am able to help. Souls farther along the path of progression can help me, and they do. Consequently, an observer may find a rescue session depressing, as all those coming through are troubled. The vast majority of people go to their loved ones immediately. I only get those who are stuck and need some help.

There is considerable interaction between the astral plane and the earth plane. Situations are created on earth which have their origin in the higher planes of awareness. A person in spirit, wishing to become a guide to someone on the earth, may require a brief earth contact to establish a link between the planes. Sometimes he will incarnate briefly to make the contact; then, he will return to spirit. In a situation like this he may be a stillborn child or a sudden infant death. The parents will be receptive to this at a higher level but they will experience much grief and growth through this experience which they have wanted. Of course, the experience would not have the same impact if those involved were aware of this apparent loss when the child came to the physical level.

It is only from the spirit world that we are able to see the broader view of the grand design of the creation. If we take the time to think about the possible reasons for some of the supposed tragedies of life, this earth plane becomes more endurable. I hear expressions like, "If spirit is love, why are children born blind or crippled?" There would be no variations of personality or free will if we were all born the same. We would be puppets on a string playing out a role for no other purpose than to please some capricious God.

From the astral plane we can see how many black people were once involved in the slave trade and how many bigots were once black. To really know what it's like to understand some experience we were once involved in, where other people suffered, we have to walk in those footsteps. There are many people, who, having gained through the suffering of others, are given the opportunity to grow by returning to earth in an appropriate situation. This is not punishment, it is an opportunity to grow, and is the choice of the individual.

Within every expression of life, from a thought to a rock, is the divine creative energy which we lovingly call our Father. So seek first the spiritual essence, and all things will become known. The exploration of the astral plane is exciting and enlightening and much can be learned from it. There is nothing to fear except our own creations on the astral plane and, if we can remember to express love to all things that threaten us, we will always be in control. No one in spirit wishes us any harm, and the great power of love will keep us clear of any self-created trouble.

For the serious student, the astral plane is obviously the next step for spiritual growth. An intense meditation on the astral energy centers will bring reactions to each level experienced. There will be a consciousness shift to the appropriate center and physical responses will be felt.

The red/physical center will bring intense physical control and concentration similar to the Hatha Yoga state of perfect physical achievement.

The orange center will bring wide swings of emotion and heightened sensitivity of the nervous system. Each emotion will be experienced spontaneously, and this may happen suddenly and sometimes inappropriately.

The yellow center may bring a wide range of feelings and intellectual acuity.

The green/astral center ranges from physical feelings of envy, possessiveness and rigidity, to flexibility and adaptability.

Following these four earth-related centers there will be a distinct change of consciousness, and the emotional levels are no longer relevant to the fifth and higher dimensions.

CHAPTER TWELVE

SPIRITUAL HEALING

SPIRITUAL HEALING IS A FORM OF MEDIUMSHIP where the healer can act as a channel for healing power from the spirit world. The healer relies on the intervention of psychic powers beyond the physical world and attempts to utilize these powers for the good of the person seeking help. The intention is to create an energy field which the patient can draw on in order to strengthen or enhance the patient's own natural healing ability.

I usually ask the patient why they have come for psychic healing, as well as what they think their problem is. I do not want a clinical diagnosis, I only want to know what the patient thinks is wrong. Sometimes I feel I should explain that healers are not doctors, and that I am merely a channel for spirit power. I want the patient to understand that it is the power and the patient, not the healer that does the healing.

Sometimes a person will come for healing of the soul and not the body. They may have suffered a loss, feel lonely, or just want to talk to someone. I recommend that any healer should use a little personal interaction, a friend-liness, and a concern for the person by showing a positive attitude to him and by being a good listener. A person may come for healing for a terminal illness to see if psychic healing can help when the medical professional has exhausted his resources. As a Hospice volunteer I meet many souls in this situation. In such cases I tell the person I will do the best I can, and he or she should not give up hope. I try not to make empty promises and advise them to have faith in their particular religious preference and the doctors who can ease any pains.

If a patient has no religious preference, I usually ask him if he has any questions about his situation, and the forthcoming transition he must make to another life. I have received some interesting atheistic or agnostic responses to my queries. Most people tell me they have made peace with the Lord and are comfortable with what is happening to them. Some people want some assurance that there is a life after this one. This prompts some discussions about the possibility of survival.

I am sometimes asked to give a prayer for the patient by the caregiver, who is usually the patient's wife, and I also alert the caregiver to the availability of grief counseling.

As the laying-on of hands is the primary method of healing in Spiritualism, I also ask a person if it is all right for me to lightly touch them. Some psychic healers would rather not touch the person but prefer to work through the auric emanation around the patient. As all spirit healing takes place in the astral plane before it manifests in the physical world, auric healing is just as effective. I find every healer develops his own method or style.

Psychic healing power is an energy drawn from higher levels of being. It is enhanced by spirit powers and is used to overcome an imbalance in the energy field of the body of the patient. The healing power comes directly from the higher spheres of the healer's spirit and flows through the healer to provide extra energy for the patient to use.

There is an incredible impulse on the part of the higher self to protect a person's physical body. This body is the spirit's representation on the earth plane and is very precious to the higher self. If both the healer and the patient can tune in to a higher state of awareness, then the whole healing process is raised to a spiritual level. It is usually beneficial to encourage the patient to raise his thoughts to a spiritual level in prayer or meditation during the healing process. Faith can produce miracles, so why not expect one.

There is an assumption by some people that all sickness is a failure on the part of the patient to correctly manifest the inner spirit here on earth. Intellectually that may be true but it is not what a patient wants to hear. Spontaneous healing by a change in the patient's beliefs would seem to bear this out, but such beliefs could lead to a patient ignoring available medical help. A combination of medical and alternative healing treatment would appear to be the best approach. It matters not who gets the credit for the healing, the important thing is the recovery of the patient. The credit for the healing belongs to the power, not the healer.

Obviously, there are some medical problems that need a doctor's attention and a healer should not try play doctor and set broken bones, etc. If a person is going for some radiation therapy I always tell them to cooperate with the procedure and to visualize the radiation as attacking the disease.

A person can call on his own inner healing power for help, and, I think, it is a good thing to explain this to the patient. I usually encourage a person to use some relaxation techniques or to learn to meditate. In this way a person can call on his own resources and feel part of the healing process. He can gain a sense of peace and confidence from his own higher self and ask for guidance and healing. Many sicknesses are stress related and stress is one condition which will respond favorably to relaxation or meditation.

I usually use an analogy to explain what I am doing when a new patient comes for healing. I tell the patient that his body is like a vehicle with a battery that has run down, and that a healer can recharge it by using some psychic/spiritual energy to help the body restore itself. If the patient is new to psychic healing, it is a good practice to ask him if he has any questions about healing as this can help the patient relax.

I always work from the back of a patient and make contact by placing my hands on the patient's shoulders. Often, I can sense areas of depletion in the patient's energy field. Conditions may be lightly mirrored on my body by a mild sensation; however, as soon as I mentally acknowledge them, they disappear. I consider this can be an indication from my guide in spirit to give emphasis to areas that may need it.

I then concentrate on the spinal column as this seems to be the distribution center for the nervous system and it is through this system that the psychic energy flows. I do not attempt to manipulate the spine as it is the inner senses that I am contacting. I think that many Chiropractors are knowingly or unwittingly combining spiritual healing with their treatments. I think a good healer is someone who has overcome the need to feel they are the power. Once they accept that it is the power that handles any corrections necessary then they can mentally step aside and allow the guides in spirit to work through them. I visualize the patient in good health and allow the healing to take place. Usually the patient will feel a flow of heat from a healer's hands, as well as a sense of relaxation during the treatment.

I always encourage, and never discourage a patient from going to a physician. To ignore many years of medical research is denying a healing resource for the patient. Similarly, to ignore alternate methods of treatment is not wise. We should use any resource in which the patient has faith and may benefit from. Sometimes, when a person is sick he has a fear that the worst may be happening and that he is going to die. At such times an unthinking remark by someone may give a sense of realism to a fear. For example, if a person feels things are hopeless and that he is a helpless victim of some circumstance, he may begin to believe the worst and experience a lot of unnecessary grief. A healer should be careful when expressing an opinion to a patient.

In many ways, good health is the result of interaction between the mind and the body. A fear will cause an imbalance in the flow of the life-force and inhibit the natural protection of the body. Fears can be overcome by self-healing or by a healing meditation. Listening to the patient and counseling can help the person realize that fear has only the power that we give it is often enough to remove the fear. When appropriate, I will try to get the patient to understand this.

The best situation for healing is with the cooperation and involvement of the patient. Healing will in all cases depend on the belief of the patient that he can be cured. It depends on the strength of purpose that the illness serves, and on the desire of the patient to get well.

Sometimes a patient will not want to get well. I have spoken with some patients who were terminally ill and some of them said they did not want to be healed. They felt they would have to go through some similar process in order to leave this life; and so, they were content to leave things alone. I have seen patients who were terminally ill being taken to healers by someone who wants them well again. Patient's may go through the motions of seeking help for the sake of a concerned relative but their hearts are not in it. In many cases the approaching death of a loved one is not a subject that families are ready to discuss.

Many of the rescue situations involve people who have died of injury or disease. The first thing I do is get them to understand that physical things stay on the earth plane, and that is especially true of the physical body and its ills. A person may imagine he is still sick; so, I will go through a simple healing procedure to make him realize it is his imagination that is causing him to hang on to the illness.

All that is necessary for the persons who are being rescued is for them to realize that we create our own reality, and that we are what we think we are. The moment they accept the suggestion that they can be free of their condition, it begins to go away. As soon as they realize the changes are because of their new beliefs, the healing process speeds up and they are quickly healed and are ready to move on into spirit.

In each level of awareness that we are able to experience, we assume the body or vehicle of expression appropriate to the vibration of that particular level. In meditation the various vibration rates can be felt as we go deeper into ourselves. The same is true in healing. I often feel a strange sense of disorientation during the process of healing and I know it is when the guides are closest to me.

Each level of consciousness has its own vibration. We can experience one example in the dream state. The time order is different, and once we are free of the time restrictions of the earth plane, we can travel freely by a change of perception. This is also true when we die. We don't go anywhere, we just see things differently by a change in perception.

I try to get the being who has died to see himself free of the body. Once he is able to do this, a new realization comes to him; then it is easy for me to get him to look into the light for the next stage of his journey.

When a person goes through the transition with a firm belief that he has an incurable disease, he will argue with me that he cannot be cured. Sometimes I will go through a healing process to restore him using nothing but suggestion. If that doesn't work, I will tell the individual that there is a healing center where he can get help; then I send him to the healers in spirit.

In the astral plane, if a person still exhibits a sickness, then it is obvious that the sufferer has accepted the illness into his self-image. He identifies himself as a victim through suggestions that he has given to himself. He has hung on to the illness and only a change in his attitude will remove it. This is a task for the rescue worker or the healers in spirit. Also, in the astral plane, an illness is seen as a failure to solve a psychological or mental problem correctly, and as long as the illness is the main focus of the person, the problem remains unsolved. As soon as the problem is identified, the attention of the patient is redirected away from the illness and it will go away.

This is true of the AIDS sufferer on earth who has been rejected by society, his own family, and some of the medical establishments. We tend to hide the sufferer in special hospitals and treat the disease as incurable. Here again, if the patient can be encouraged to use self-healing, as well as the medical treatment, he will automatically cooperate with the healer and assist in the healing process.

Eventually, when the person goes to spirit, he will realize that any sickness is curable by a change in his self-perception. I believe that all miraculous healing by a rescue worker is done by the patient coming to the realization of his own higher power. There have been cases where a cancer patient has been cured completely by the use of self-help even on the earth plane.

Counseling and guidance are helpful in any treatment program and, regardless of the type of treatment, concern for the welfare of the patient is always beneficial. Most people in the healing professions are concerned with the well-being of their clients, otherwise the practitioner would soon become burned out.

I remind healers that they will benefit from the healing as much as the patient. We cannot run water through a hose without the hose getting wet, and healing power running through a healer will benefit the healer as well.

There are still many questions about the nature of illness, its sources and its cures. Whatever the cause of sickness of any kind, the best way is for a healer to ignore the arguments and treat the effects. Compassion and concern for the welfare of another person will enhance the flow of healing power to the patient and that cannot be bad for either the patient or the healer.

CHAPTER THIRTEEN

WHAT IS REALITY?

SCIENTISTS TELL US we live in a world of energy which manifests in form according to the configuration and vibration of the atoms in the substance. For example, we can take something solid like a piece of ice, apply energy to it in the form of heat, and it becomes a liquid. Continue to apply the same energy and it becomes a gas called steam. The steam can be separated into oxygen and hydrogen; so, if sufficient energy is applied to the hydrogen atom, it will be found to consist of nothing but energy. At which level is reality? Obviously, reality depends on the conditions to which the substance is exposed.

We see this world of vibrating energy as if it is real. However, science again informs us that the universe we see is energy vibrating at thirty-three vibrations per second and that our physical faculties are programmed to interact at the same rate. If our senses are disturbed, and if we are not in synchronization, then the world disappears from our view, or we transfer our awareness to another dimension.

It seems that we all see reality in our own terms and no two people see the same things in quite the same way. A good example of this is to visit an art gallery with a group of people and listen to the opinions of different people and compare them with your own. We tend to project our preferences on to every observation.

As we have distinctly different ideas of who we are, then it seems that we create our own ideas of what is real. It would appear that the reality we create is the projection of our ideas on to this energy field we call earth or the third dimension.

The world does seem to have certain constant factors that we observe when we are born. As we grow, we evaluate these factors and create our own personality by reacting to the influences exerted upon us from the environment. The world was here before we arrived here; so, there has to be some durability to it.

Upon entry into this world, we adopt the language of the culture, and we are restricted by the limitations of the language when we wish to communicate. Beautiful as many languages are, some terms which we fully understand here on earth are invalid outside of this dimension. For example, when describing progressive steps of development we use the words "plane" and "level," and we know what we mean. In the spirit world they do not apply. The only differences I have observed in those states of awareness are merely variations of the vibration rate to which we respond as the observer.

The atmosphere is an energy field vibrating according to the particular level we are in, and our ideas create what we see as reality. We create observable phenomenon by some kind of unconscious thought projection which causes the thoughts to read time and place. Reality for us is an idea we have in concert with others.

When we enter this world, we accept its limitations and restrictions, and we create or contribute to its reality. Our higher self projects an image into this energy field in the form of an incarnation seed. This seed contains the pattern we have selected for this incarnation and is our link with the infinite.

The fact that we are born means we have to interact with the environment. We naturally have free will and this allows us to accept change which causes growth and development. This act of creation by the higher self means we have the life force within us that is necessary to maintain an image here in this dimension. There is a similarity with the seed becoming the flower, or the acorn becoming the oak tree.

In rescue work, I send people on to a light that they see ahead of them. They see it after I direct them to it, and if it is the emanation of love from the advanced beings which attracts those in transition, it must mean the higher beings are always available. When a person arrives in the vibration of the light he is automatically attracted to those beings who have come to meet him. Together they begin to reproduce a living situation in which the desires of the newcomer are gratified. So, we create our own interpretation of reality in each level that we express ourselves. The world is my idea.

When I am dealing with souls in transition, those who reject help and refuse to interact with the guides and others will recreate some past experience in which they feel secure. This usually means they are still in their home or hospital situation and will try to continue with their previous life and influence their surroundings. They find that other people cannot interact with them and then they can become very angry. If they have guilt over past negative behavior they may create an atmosphere of darkness around themselves. They think that if they cannot see they cannot be seen.

It appears we apply our free will after we are born, and use our ideas of who we think we are, to determine the person we become. Of course, there are some predetermined factors, such as genetic heritage, which have a definite influence on our lives in this dimension. In fact, there is a school of thought that suggests we bring information from previous existences which has a subtle influence on this life. I think that is doubtful, if a situation has already been experienced, there is no point in re-living it. Actions or circumstances from a previous existence may help determine a trend for a future life experience, but each life is a completely new experience.

So, many people try to make reincarnation or Karma an excuse for what is happening in this life. Some people think they have to pay in this life for something that happened in another life, but that is not so.

When we come in to this life we have already chosen how long we will remain, and how we will die at the end of it. Many persons do not know how they have been killed, they have no memory of it, so how can they reproduce it for another life.

All reincarnation beliefs are applicable to the earth plane and the astral plane only and have no significance in the spirit world. Reincarnation is a belief system for people who do not understand that time is a self-created illusion, which we use to measure the experience of consciousness in this dimension.

This explanation of what the world consists of, raises many questions as to who we are. Are we born with a blank slate on which we are writing the script of our lives, or is there some prescribed pattern of behavior we have to follow? The blank slate theory would mean we have complete freedom to do whatever we like. The predetermination theory would mean we are just puppets. Perhaps there are elements of both in our make-up.

Physicists and chemists have their scientific model of approach to these questions of the creation of the universe, but somehow the answers seem to be within ourselves. If we would introspect and shift our focus of consciousness away from the external world, we would find realms of thought patterns or worlds that seem as real as this world seems to be.

It was at this stage of self-realization that I decided to explore who I am through the channels of religion. I looked into a variety of religions from Christianity to Eastern Religions as well as some ancient ideas of what reality is. From my studies, and an investigation of different approaches to the truth, I finally realized that Spiritualism was closer to the truth I was seeking. The more I studied this variation of Christian thinking, the more I realized there are some answers to these questions I had. Apparently it is true that the truth is within us. This statement appears in almost every religious philosophy, and the only difference seems to be in the approach used to find the truth. In Spiritualism the approach is to extend our sensitivity to incorporate other states of awareness and to gain knowledge from discarnate entities. Spirit has been a wonderful source of information, not only of life after death, but also knowledge of how things came to be in this world.

The principles of Spiritualism emphasize survival beyond this life, and that the universe is the result of an Infinite Intelligence, and that no soul is ever lost. Spiritualism teaches that there are specially trained or gifted individuals called mediums or sensitives who have the ability to communicate with other states of awareness.

From many years of investigation into these claims I have to agree completely with their philosophy. I have had sittings with a wide variety of mediums over the past fifty years and I have been given irrefutable proof of these claims of immortality.

One belief system that creates as lot of confusion is reincarnation. The common belief in a lineal procession of lives is a workable system for people who have difficulty accepting or understanding simultaneous time. All that has been, will be, and is, is now. All that is, was created at one moment and we select a point of awareness and create a time frame to experience it.

We are locked in a belief of the past, present and future and usually look to the past when talking about reincarnation. In simultaneous time the future has already been lived but our attention is in this third dimension exclusively. I firmly believe that the future is now, in a higher vibration, and will manifest when we can tune into it. Some mystics and mediums are able to touch this higher vibration briefly.

It is quite possible for anyone to reach the conclusion that there is another life after this one, and as long as a person uses common sense, the quest for truth will be enlightening and very rewarding.

In every religious ideology there are people who are on some ego trip to gain some personal aggrandizement or notoriety. There are also some people who are out to mislead or extort money from the gullible. I do advise that a seeker finds a reliable teacher who is not out for money in order to guide you through the early stages of your search. Sometimes when the student is ready a teacher appears, as if it is all planned.

Any spiritualist church or group is a good place to start. Then a person's own quest for truth will lead him to the right teachers and to this force of unconditional love which we call God.

CHAPTER FOURTEEN

THE DREAM STATE

IN SPIRITUALISM our beliefs include an acceptance of other states of consciousness. We are constantly faced with questions about what is real in this world, as well as in these other states of consciousness. Apart from the normal physical level of awareness, we can extend our consciousness to the one level that is very close to this one and that, of course, is the dream state.

I think it is obvious that the dream experience is a mental activity, similar to the normal mind action on the brain. Going from one state to the other is merely a redirection of the focus of our attention. So the dream state can be described as a mind-state where all physical objects are absent.

Normally our attention is outer-directed, but we do have the ability to withdraw our attention and change our perception to a different level. Going from waking to sleeping is such an example.

When we begin to study dream states, a number of questions immediately come to mind. For example, where are these dream locations? We dream of houses and streets, and we can see for miles in our dream. Where is that space or distance? Is there a difference between a house on earth and the same house seen in a dream? If one house is a reproduction of the other, which one is real? If the dreamer is creating one house, does he create both?

Occurrences there can cover years of normal earth experience in a few minutes of earth-time. There is obviously a distortion of space/time as we know it on earth, and, I think, it is related to variations in the energy vibration that is the basis of all matter.

What is the composition of the objects we see in our dreams? If this is a mental experience, are we creating the whole thing and do other people we see in our dreams share the same experience that we do?

When we return to this state of awareness there seems to be a distortion of time as we know it on earth. People I contact in rescue work are very confused as to earth time. I have had people from the middle ages who think they have been in spirit a few weeks. Some people are astounded by the passage of time since they have died. I tell young children that their parents will be with them soon, knowing that the time differential will enable them to accept the separation from their parents.

The dream world is always there when we sleep, regardless of the time of day. This fact alone helps us to see that the activity in the dream state keeps pace with us in this world. It is as if there is a parallel universe which we can enter when free of the physical body.

The dream world is not some imaginary place; rather, it is a world of ideas, thoughts, and mental activity out of which we create scenarios that react to our thoughts. Emotions are very real and we experience the same rapid changes of fear and love as when we are awake.

It is possible for a person to develop the ability to experience the dream state consciously while still in a physical body. This is known as astral projection and is practiced by many mystics and others who bring back information about the conditions in this altered state of consciousness.

We have extra powers in the dream state, and we are able to resolve many emotional problems such as anger and fear in our dreams. The dream world and the physical world are very closely related, and we have our memory in both levels so that we can maintain our sense of identity. In fact, there is not a time when we are not a being with a personality and a sense of beingness.

One of the dream level powers we can use is freedom of travel. We can explore other realms of being while the body sleeps and can learn much about the nature of beingness in other higher levels of consciousness. We have only to think of a place we would like to see and we are there. Apparently we do not go anywhere. We merely change our perception and observe the recreation of a situation based on our memory or expectation of what we wish to observe.

One of the big questions arising out of inter-dimensional study is whether all states of awareness are merely thought forms created by the image-creating ability of the mind. Some scholars and scientists maintain that we enter into every observation and the world is, because we are. Would the world exist if there were no observers, in the same way that the dream world ceases to exist consciously when we awaken?

The deeper we are able to penetrate into the origin of matter, we are able to realize that the universe is a mass of energy manifesting according to the laws of the vibration level where it is. The same must be true of the dream state.

Regardless of how many times we can reduce the atom, we are always faced with the truth that we are merely using different words to describe the basic creative energy of the universe. We can have a perfectly logical existence in other states, such as the dream world; so it is impossible to think of oneself as being dead because we are always supposing there is an observer.

Most dreams are the result of memories from the past few days and most dream interpretation is based on what has transpired recently in the life of the dreamer. This may be a help to a counselor treating a patient, but I feel that no one can really tell the meaning of a dream as well as the person having the experience, if they can look at it objectively.

Many times, dreams are the result of suppressed emotions. Dreams can release us from many fears by transferring the fear to some related scenario in the astral plane.

Many people have had predictive dreams where they have been able to see the future. Every detail of a future experience is played out and the dreamer is an active participant in what is happening. This gives rise to the big question: If it is possible to see the future in the dream state, are we merely following a prescribed life script? Is there really free will or is there predestination?

The guides in spirit tell me we have laid out a pattern to our lives that appears to have been laid out for us. With our full cooperation, before we are born into this dimension, we decide the framework of our life to come. Within those guidelines there is free will as to whether to follow the pattern or not. Even when a situation has been seen ahead in the dream state it can be changed. Some people have had a warning of a pending disaster and have been able to avoid it. Some people have had a feeling that they should not board a plane or a ship that has met with disaster. These experiences are not just coincidences.

Until I came into Spiritualism, I thought that dreams were the result of the subconscious mind acting up in the sleep state. Subsequent studies have lead me to understand that the dream state is another level of expression of the creative essence. It certainly allows us to explore another level of consciousness and to realize that the earth experience is not all that there is.

In the dream state there is some rescue work performed by people who are also living on the earth plane. I have many recollections of experience in other realms and have been in some interesting situations, some of which were uncomfortable. If I became too involved in an experience on the lower planes, I found I could identify with, and become attached very easily.

I have been in some of the lower levels and have tried to get people there to change their perspective. Sometimes it can be done, but often I have been unsuccessful.

There are planes where sex dominates and groups of beings are working out their hang-ups. There are planes of anger and violence and the people there are always ready to drive away anyone who is trying to help them. The rescue worker has to keep in mind that he is immortal and indestructible and ignore any attempts to attack him.

There is no heaven or hell in the astral planes unless it is self-created. A person believing in a hell and expecting to go there, will manifest his expectation in whatever terms he thinks he deserves. If a person expects some God to punish him, he will look for someone, or something to carry it out. In this situation, it is usually easy for a rescue worker to redirect the person's attention and send him on to spirit.

The guides, helpers and rescue workers try only to encourage progression for everyone; however, there are many who have found a home in their new situation. Of course, the whole idea of negativity is a value judgment and people can only be led, not forced to comply to another's standards.

It does not require much imagination to visualize what can be created by the memories of some of the fearful beings in these planes. There are people who have lived lives of desolation when they were on the earth; so, they would naturally recreate the same situation in a place where they can create what they wish.

One big question that the rescue worker is faced with is, do we have the right to try to change the life style of those who have chosen to live in their own way? Somewhere inside us there is an instinct that tells us what is better for all of us and we can only hope we do the right thing when working with those in other planes.

I have found that in all the helping professions and in spiritual healing and rescue work, the question of interference is resolved by helping the people realize their potential and helping them to decide what is best for themselves. Sometimes they need a little nudge to wake up to what their potential is.

The dream world brings out many interesting questions for us to ponder. The guides in spirit have answers to these questions and I have had much help in understanding the laws of this next plane of awareness.

On some of the out-of-body excursions I still react as I would on the earth plane until I remember where I am, and that I am indestructible. This helps me to understand how it is that a person in the astral plane can feel all the emotions we know here on earth.

The range of experiences in the astral plane extend from the lowest and most desolate to the spirit world where only love can live. I have found that we are attracted to the level that reflects our emotional needs. Once we outgrow these needs we can progress to other levels of awareness, not just the astral plane.

Love is the key. To be able to love oneself and others is the most difficult yet most rewarding achievement in any state of consciousness. We can use love as a protection against our own fear of others in a dream situation. This astral plane or dream state provides the means whereby this can be proven.

CHAPTER FIFTEEN

THE HUMAN AURA

SURROUNDING THE PHYSICAL BODY is an energy field, generally known as the aura. It is an emanation from both
the physical state of consciousness and the next level,
known as the astral plane. In reality there are no planes or
levels. There are only variations in the rate of vibration of
the universal energy that is present at every expression of
the creative essence, or wherever an individual is focussed.
However, for the purpose of this discussion it is easier to
use the terms which convey a meaning which we all understand.

All objects are composed of an energy which is constantly moving and radiating into our range of vision for us
to see. All forms are the result of this energy and we are able
to see this as a band of light around objects. This light is one
of the parts of the aura.

Around any inanimate object such as a rock, this band
of light is seen. Around all living things, including vegeta-
tion, animals and human beings, the aura varies in extent,
density and color. The brightness of the colors are determined by the emotions of the person and are constantly
changing, as are the emotions. Also the aura can be affected

by another person who can project his ideas onto this vibration of energy. This is part of our sensory mechanism and we may be able to feel the presence of other beings in close proximity through the sensitivity of the auric atmosphere without the use of the usual five physical senses.

Everything in this third dimension is currently vibrating at the rate of approximately thirty-three vibrations per second. This enables all life forms, including people, to have a similar world-view. Any change in the vibration rate, as seen by an observer will cause a loss of compatibility between the observer and this third dimension and will bring disorientation and possibly, loss of consciousness.

Some people are able to see these auras when they are in tune with the astral vibration and so, a spontaneous vision of an aura is not unusual. At times of extreme emotion, the metabolic rate of the observer increases and the possibility of psychic vision is heightened.

The aura is something here for our physical and astral levels. The aura is not important when you leave these two planes, because there is no such thing in higher states of awareness. We do not have the same emotions in the higher states of consciousness as they have been outgrown and only love prevails. After these two levels of awareness we enter what is known as the fifth dimension, where we become part of everything around us.

Then there is only a clear and loving light that we project, and that intensifies as we grow into higher levels of greater understanding. This earthly/astral aura becomes clearer and brighter as we progress, changing the colors until they become the light which is pure unconditional love.

The vibration rate of those beings that come from a higher plane is so different, so much stronger, that we could not handle the power upon this plane. They do not even come here to try to contact us directly, and they must go through another being at a less advanced level to act as a medium or channel. Otherwise, we would have to increase our rate of vibration so that our vision is compatible with theirs.

Sometimes in meditation or out-of-body experience it is possible to be drawn into a level of awareness where a higher being can be seen. This is rare, the higher beings will usually assume a form we can relate to and lower their vibration to communicate with us on the earth plane. They do this in order to inspire us to raise our consciousness closer to their level.

The aura becomes the purest when we reach a higher level of the astral plane. It is determined by the state of being that we are in, and we have emotions here on the earth plane that do not exist there. Once beyond the astral plane such things as fear and anger no longer persist as these are outgrown on this emotion/desire plane.

The colors that we see here and on the astral plane, are perceived until we enter what could be termed several levels above the third dimension, well above where we are on the earth plane. The colors come basically with the soul or being that comes to the earth plane to begin life here. Everything here on earth is a living thing, whether it be a solid rock or a breath of air.

On the earth plane we have an atmosphere that transforms energy from the sun into light and color. In the spirit world such conditions do not apply as the basic energy is part of the creative essence and all power comes from within.

This pure light surrounding us at the higher levels of consciousness becomes less bright as we enter into the slower vibrations of the astral and physical worlds. It transforms into the colors of the aura and into the physical energy required for it to express itself in human form.

Within all form is this creative essence which we see as light and is the divine spark, or God, or whatever name is in vogue.

The powerful spirit and psychic energy comes from within all things. It is in the very center of all atomic activity. It is this energy that creates the aura and becomes the present colors we can see. We are perceiving this activity through human eyes that give it color. So, when we raise our vibration to a different level we see with our inner senses and we see some colors that are not known on the earth plane.

If we look at a tree, it is capable of a certain auric color, because it has within its auric field the different energies that are required for it to be a tree. If it does not have enough water or nutrients or sunlight, the colors in the aura of the tree is affected because the tree is a living thing.

If we look at a cat or a dog, its aura is a little more complex than a tree, it has some emotional feelings, but not to the extent that a human has. We have many more emotions and feelings. It is we humans that have the most developed aura as far as colors are concerned. When we look with our psychic eye, or third eye, to see an aura, we can see that all auras are different. Some are larger and more colorful than others,

When looking psychically at a person we may see a beautiful light around them when other people will think that he is not a good person. The difference is in the eye of the beholder. We could look at everyone and see only the good within their aura, and we would not see any of the negativity in the person. Our perception can be very selective and it is natural for us to perceive things from the level where we are conscious.

There are people who can see the aura and see what is considered to be a medical problem, and that is all they see. They do not see other things around the person. Some healers look for the radiation of energy in the aura of a patient. They can tell from the brightness of the colors and from changes in the intensity of the radiation from within the patient where there are areas in need of attention. It is as if rays of radiation from the aura of the patient sag where there is sickness, or disharmony.

There are some people who feel they can get information about a person's past and future by looking at an aura. In view of the rapid changing nature of the aura, and the emotions that create it, such information is doubtful at best. A good psychic can tell the present emotional state of a subject by observing the aura, and use that as a focal point to explore other levels of a subject's nature.

The colors emitted from the various energy centers seem to vary in response to the emotional feelings of the person. Into our everyday language we find there are similar references to this phenomenon. We use such expressions as, "Red with anger, Yellow with fear, and Green with envy." These are the negative aspects of the colors which usually manifest in darker shades. The positive aspects are bright, flashing colors. The red color becomes pink and denotes spiritual love. The bright yellow denotes expertise in the use of intuition and the intellect. The bright green shows generosity and flexibility.

There are various levels of the astral plane and at the higher levels each person has a steady auric color which depicts the person's basic temperament. An emotional, feeling person will have a bright orange color and an intellectual person will have a yellow color. These basic colors may change during a lifetime as the person progresses spiritually, but only slightly.

The aura is an astral plane activity and is one of the planes of consciousness between the physical and spirit worlds. It is part of the creative process and is a link with the higher dimensions of our being. As such it is a microcosm of the total expression of the divine emanation of the life force in man.

As this creative force becomes man, these links between the levels of being are established. They provide an avenue to the higher expressions of the self. From the physical center at the base of the spine, to the link with the infinite at the crown of the head, there is this channel that can bring knowledge of the higher self to the seeker on the earth plane.

These links are through the inner senses and are discussed more fully in Chapters 9 and 11.

CHAPTER SIXTEEN

CONCLUSION

M ANY SIGNIFICANT CONCLUSIONS have come from my
studies and from the psychic and spiritual development I have had with various teachers, both on earth and
from spirit. The undeniable truth of survival beyond this
life must rank high in any list of important discoveries for
anyone new to religion, as I was when I began.

As my concepts of reality changed, so did my attitudes
and my appreciation of the love and guidance I received
from those in spirit. I would encourage anyone who feels
inspired or feels the need to find truth and love within
himself to raise his awareness or consciousness to the next
dimension.

Looking back over the past fifty years, I can see a slow
unfolding of inner truths that have made me the person
devoted to service that I have become and which has
fulfilled my life.

One significant revelation that has come from the
rescue work (that I have been involved with for the last
eighteen years) is that we create our own reality wherever
we are by the thoughts that we think. These thoughts are
the result of our reaction to, or interaction with, whatever

environment we are in. We create our interpretation of this world experience, and share it with others who are within the same range of vibration. The fact that we are born demands that we interact with the environment.

It is as if the combined thoughts of everyone who has ever lived in this dimension, has shared in the creation of the universe according to the divine plan we are interpreting.

There are as many interpretations of reality as there are beings who are conscious and capable of thought, for reality is an idea in the mind of the observer which is shared by everyone in this dimension at this time. Other dimensions seem to be as real as the earth plane, as evidenced in the dream experience or in any other out-of-body excursions.

In rescue work on several occasions I have had information from people in distress in the astral plane of the spirit world before the news of their death was made public. Victims of capital crimes can be brought to a rescue worker soon after their transition to spirit, and they can move on into the spirit world before their earthly disappearance is known. Practically every situation that comes through for help, is further evidence of survival of the human spirit beyond the grave.

The joyous reunions of souls who, after being trapped, are freed to go to their loved ones who are waiting for them has been one of the pleasures of this work. The release of people who thought that nobody cared for them or where they were has also been rewarding. The greatest joy, however, has been the opportunity to heal those who believe they are still sick, and to watch them recreate themselves by a change in their beliefs.

Another great truth is that we only take our memory and character with us into the next life. This means that life in the next dimension is a continuation; so, we have to outgrow the old ideas of reality that we have formed on earth. We have to outgrow any attachments we have formed. This applies to things like money, property, religion and other earthbound concepts that have no value in the spirit world.

I firmly believe that there is a force of creative energy that manifests as consciousness. This essence of creativity is felt as love and is the basic energy that is within all things. This force is known as God to most people, and, if God can be accepted as a force and not as a super being, then it is true that God is love.

Raising any subject or concept such as philosophy, science, mathematics or any human study to a higher level will eventually be found to be based in the essence of love. One surgeon remarked that there is often a time when he is operating when some higher power seems to take over from him, and guide him through a difficult situation.

Mankind interprets this creative force and is constantly seeking self-fulfillment by making real this impulse to express himself.

I know that no one is ever completely lost forever. As we choose our own reality, we can dwell in an imaginary world in the astral plane for as long as we choose to resist the impulse to move on into higher realms of experience. There are many souls in the next plane who are willing to help all who come from the earth plane. However, we must ask for help and be willing to accept the guidance offered by those who are waiting to receive us.

I have found that contrary to many ideas, there is no judgment or punishment for past actions except the guilt that comes from the realization that we have created who we are. Many times a return to the earth plane is an attempt to put right some of the wrongs from the past and improve ones self concept.

Love is the basis of life in the spirit world and once free of attachment to the earth plane, we come to an understanding of the truth that love is there for all of us to use or abuse. This is one of the things that is difficult for us to accept on the earth plane.

I know there are great beings ahead of mankind who are on the spiritual path and who have a tremendous power of love in all levels of awareness. Yet I also know they do not want to be worshipped or adored, for they are only too willing to help us in our quest to be like them. They know that one day we will be at their level.

All these concepts can be realized as a result of meditation and by raising our awareness to a higher level. There are no secrets in the spirit world; so, there is nothing to fear as death or the transition to the spirit world is a release not a punishment.

I hope this book will answer some questions about the after-life and help those who are seeking a broader concept of reality. There is nothing to fear in the next dimensions as long as you remember you are indestructible and fear is a product of the earth and its superstitions.

Raising ones consciousness to the God force and seeking the love from spirit is all anyone needs to find themselves. So seek ye first the kingdom and all will be revealed.

* * * * *

I have decided to include a list of the more common types of cases that have come for help through the years. The reader must keep in mind that a person dies with a picture in his mind and a belief in his last experience and they have difficulty realizing the transition they have made.

Children:

> Lost in the woods or runaways dying of exposure.
>
> Hiding from parents because of fear of punishment. They are usually tired of repeated beatings.
>
> Locked in a refrigerator by accident or childish play.
>
> Locked in closets as a form of punishment.
>
> Killed by predators after molestation. Many kidnap victims.
>
> Killed by parents or other relatives in a fit of anger.
>
> Killed by parent during or following incest.
>
> Children unable to breathe when smothered.
>
> Suicide to punish parents, or guilt concerning misbehavior.
>
> Suicide from despair or disenchantment with life.

Adults:

> Dying in nursing homes, hospitals and other institutions.
>
> Suicide. Desperation with situation in life. Sickness and pain making life intolerable. Guilt following taking the life of another, especially a child.
>
> Self-destructive behavior with drugs, alcohol, or recklessness.
>
> Murdered in prison by guards or other inmates. Dying in extended solitary confinement.
>
> Gang warfare, drive-by shootings and drug activities.
>
> Gang members killed by the gang for lack of loyalty.
>
> Skid row and the homeless people who die in back alleys.
>
> Police officers killed in line of duty, sometimes seeking revenge.
>
> Buried by mine cave-in or snow avalanche.
>
> Bitten by snakes. One man thought he could reach his snake bite kit in his pick-up.

Adults from the South who handle and worship poisonous snakes wanting to know why God didn't protect them.

Falling from buildings or trees.

Drowning. Many flood victims.

Dying in fires. Sometimes attempting rescues.

Road accidents. Cars, motorcycles, pedestrians.

Mass deaths. Holocaust, ethnic cleansing, ship or plane accidents.

Service men from wars dating from the Civil War to modern day from all three branches of the service.

Women:

Murdered following rape in case she talked.

Several prostitutes killed by users or pimps.

Murdered by spouse for financial gain or following arguments.

Cancer of all kinds.

Dying in loneliness after a loved one dies. Loneliness seems to be one of the most common maladies.

* * * * *

There have been many thousands of cases in a never-ending stream of people whose only problem was a lack of knowledge of the afterlife.

If people could just remember to look straight out ahead of themselves when they leave this earth and concentrate on the bright light up ahead they would find their way home to the spirit world. Remember there is nothing but love once you leave the earth/astral planes.

The truth that there is no punishment for sin will come as a surprise to offenders when they reach the other side. Having to live with the realization of who they are and what they have become is an enduring punishment. But all is for growth and eventually we leave behind the memory of the past and go on to greater things.

I asked a guide once why not instill in people before they are born the knowledge of the after life then mankind would behave differently. He responded that the future generations on earth will be indoctrinated with more spiritual values.

Despite the lust for power and wealth in politics and business, the prevalence of fear and anger in the world, I firmly believe that mankind is on a course of spiritual and intellectual progression. Without such hope there would not be the attraction to come to this planet for growth and experience.

May the great ones that I serve grant unto us all a glorious blessing.

RESCUING SOULS FROM THE WORLD TRADE CENTER (WTC)

When the terrorists' planes crashed into the WTC, thousands of people were suddenly killed and the incident was obviously a terrible shock to the victims, and to the world.

On the following day I began to receive victims of that tragedy. They were brought through the mediums I work with by my spirit guides, during my regular sessions. My job is to help them realize their new situation and get them to tell me what their problem is. Once their problem is resolved I send them on to the light up ahead of them. There they are met and helped by their family and friends who have preceded them into spirit.

The first person through was a fireman who said, "There's a lot of people here who need help and I can't get the door open." I asked him who he was and he said his name was Adam and he was a fireman from the eighth ladder company in Manhattan. I guessed he was in the WTC and he was trapped by the collapse of one of the buildings. He confirmed he was in building number two of the WTC. He said, "I can see through the windows and there are many people there but I can't get to them."

I explained to him that the building had collapsed and it was his memory that made him believe he could see anything on the earth plane. I got him to understand the situation and directed him to look up into the light. He said he could see some of his buddies from the service and some of his relatives.

I asked him to direct all the people with him there to go to the light and he should follow them when they were gone. He said he would and he told people around him to go. Then he said he would stay there and look for others, now that he knew how to help them.

When the people looked up to the light they said they could see the blue sky. Their bodies were trapped under many feet of rubble and they did not realize that they were looking into the next world.

The following day a child came through, I asked her name and she said it was Chris. She said she was with all the other kids. I asked her what had happened and she said that something had popped outside, then it got hot. I asked her if it was the WTC and she said, "That's where my mummy works."

I said, "Is this a child care center in the WTC?

She said, "Yes, this is where my mummy works and she comes to see me at lunchtime."

I said, "Chris, are there many children there with you?"

She said, "There's not as many as usual."

I said, "How old are you?" She said she was four.

I said, "Chris, I want you to look straight up ahead of you and you will see a very beautiful lady there. She is surrounded by light and has a lot of children with her, can you see her?"

She said, "Yes, I see her. She's very beautiful."

I said, "Is your mummy there?"

She said "No."

I said, "I want you to go over there to Sister Mary, that's who that lady is, and she will look after you until your mummy gets here."

Chris said, "She's crying."

I said, "If there's any other children, let me talk to them all and have them go to Sister Mary also, she can take care of you all. Chris, are they going?"

She said, "They're all leaving me alone."

I said, "You go with them, don't be left alone."

They all went to be cared for by wonderful spirit workers. I once asked Sister Mary why she always came for the children and she said, "I have hundreds of helpers to greet and care for the children, I just come for them." The children often think Sister Mary is an angel. She is always surrounded by light and she radiates love to them. There is a wonderful sense of peace and serenity with her.

The following day a man came through who had a heavy foreign accent. I had trouble getting him to talk. I asked his name and he said he was Abullah. He said he was supposed to go to heaven.

I said, "Do you know that you died?"

He said, "I know I died, I wanted to die, I planned to die, I took over the plane, I hit the World Trade Center."

I said, "You did a lot of damage, 6,000 innocent people have died there. That's a terrible burden you are carrying now."

He said, "Yes, I realize that now. I did not know this, I did not know what would happen. Oh my goodness sakes. I will have to talk it over. Who can I talk it over with?"

I said, "You can talk to me, what is your full name?"

He said, "Abullah Admeeror." (it sounded like)

I said, "Abdul, I want you to look up ahead and tell me what you see, you should see a beautiful light shining down on you."

He said, "They won't let me be anywhere?"

I said, "Yes they will, you were merely an instrument following orders. As a matter of fact there has been a shock wave throughout the world and it has united Americans into a great force against terrorism."

He was very distressed about what he had done so I directed him again to the light and asked him what he could see and he said, "I see many, many ancestors, will they accept me?"

I said, "Yes, of course they will, they understand more than we do about the reasons for this kind of thing, go over to them now."

He said "Thank you," and left.

I checked the list of names of the terrorists and this man was obviously Abdulaziz Alomari.

The next contact from the WTC was a woman and she seemed hesitant about speaking as she obviously very confused. After a while she said her name was Bonnie aged 37.

She said, "I can smell smoke and fire."

I said, "Were you trapped in a fire, where were you, in what town?" No answer.

I said, "Bonnie, you were killed in that fire, but there is no death, you are now in the spirit world. You still think you are in that fire, you are free now." No response.

I said, "Bonnie I want you to look straight up ahead," She interrupted saying, "I can't, if I look up I will see my friend and she is on fire."

I said, "Now listen to me, there is no fire anymore. It is out and you and your friend are now in the spirit world. If you will look up you will see her and see that the fire is out." I said, "Were you in New York, in the WTC?"

She said "Yes."

I said, "Bonnie listen to me, you were killed in a terrorism attack, that is what it was, and you were killed. A plane flew into the building, exploded, and a lot of people got killed. Now look up ahead and see if your friend is there."

She said, "I don't know where to go."

I had difficulty getting her to stop crying and settle down. I said, "I'm just about to tell you, Bonnie, look up into that light and there will be people waiting to meet you. Just think of yourself being there and you will be. There may be relatives there and friends, people who love you, have a look and tell me who is there."

She said, "My grandmother is there."

I said, "That's good, I wanted one relative to come and meet you, so go over to her, give her a big hug and she will look after you. God bless you dear."

One day a man came through, I asked his name and he said "They call me Bishop."

I asked him if he was a Bishop and he said, "No I'm not."

I asked him why he was called Bishop, "Are you very religious?" and he said "Yeah kind of. I'm a street preacher, and they call me the Bishop."

I said, "Were you run over or was there some accident."

He said "All I remember is a big explosion."

I said, "Where were you?"

He said, "I was in the street, I live in the street. I don't know what happened."

I found out he was from New York and he was near the WTC when the explosion took place. I told him that two planes had flown into the WTC and the buildings collapsed. He said "Noooo." I told him he was now in spirit and on his way to heaven. I joked and told him there was a vacancy up there for a Bishop and he could go there.

He said. "How nice, I didn't know that, I doubt if there's any one in need there."

I got him to look up into the light and he claimed there wouldn't be any relatives there for him as he didn't fit into the family. When he looked up he saw his Grandmother had come to meet him, so he went to her. Before he left I had him tune into anyone else there and he said there were many who went over with him.

On another occasion a man called Peter came from the Pentagon. He had been standing in the hallway and he was lost as he thought someone had turned out the lights and he was in darkness.

I told him that a plane had crashed into the Pentagon and he had been killed. He said there was no one else there with him, there had been but they had gone. When I got him to look at the light he saw his mother and other family members and he went to join them.

A man came through who did not give his name. He said he was in the WTC and there were many people there with him. I tuned him in to the light and also talked to the others and got them all to go over. He gave a running commentary as he sent people over, he said there were many people going over.

I usually exchange first names so I will have an idea who I am talking to. I have no idea at first who is there until they speak. If they do not wish to give their name, I don't pursue it. Many people who think they have done wrong are suspicious of me, especially people in prison.

The next person from the WTC was a man named Jeff, he was on the tenth floor. He also had a lot of people with him. I managed to get them all to look up and go over. Jeff was getting them to go over as if he was directing traffic. I thanked him for his help and he left.

On October 16 during a regular session I decided to start asking people from the WTC their full name. Normally I am not involved with the people to that extent as it takes extra time to get their full name and I have no use for that information. I usually ask their name as a means of introduction and try to get them to respond.

A girl aged 27 came through and said her name was Stella Marin. She had been sitting at her desk in the WTC and the windows were blown in on her. I explained what had happened and she went over to meet several members of her family.

Then came a young man of 15. He said he had been riding his skateboard and there was a big explosion and he was choked with dust and could not breathe. He had been in the vicinity of the WTC and still had his skateboard. He said his full name was Michael Henderson. I asked him to look around and see if anyone needed help and he said there was a lot of people. I enlisted his help and he said they were all following his directions. When I tuned him in, he saw his grandmother and went to her.

A young woman came through who said she was standing by a window and that was all she knew. She had no idea where she was, except that she was in the WTC. I told her that a plane had hit the building and she was now in spirit. She said her name was Mary Montgomery and when I tuned her in to the light she saw her boss. I asked his name and she said it was Richard Callahan or Mc Cullen. I sent her to him. On this occasion I did not have a tape recorder switched on, so the names are from memory.

This record of the WTC victims is up to October 23. I'm sure there will be many more coming through. All the people will be helped to contact loved ones already in spirit and my work will continue. There are always many souls in need of guidance. I wish I could get all people to realize the truth that violence is one emotion that holds us back from spiritual progression.

Printed in the United States
15562LVS00002B/1-27